ST   GRUMPY
AFTER ALL THESE YEARS

STILL GRUMPY
AFTER ALL THESE YEARS

by the creator of Grumpy Old Men
STUART PREBBLE

Cover photo by Chris Lobina

Book design by Wordzworth
www.wordzworth.com

For Alex and Jonnie

Contents

06.04.2024

I am pushing along a wheel-barrow full of horse manure from the local stables up a slight slope towards our allotment. It's part of the joy of growing vegetables on our own plot that we produce most of our compost. This is the third journey this morning and it feels like heavy going when a sharp twinge of pain flickers across my upper chest. My father died aged 75 and I am 72, and these days any time I experience an unexpected pain, I find myself thinking, "I wonder if this is it." If it is it, I wonder how the story of my demise will be related. Maybe dying while pushing horse-shit uphill will feel like something of a metaphor for a life served in television. "At least he was doing something he loved." I consider the thought and decide that I'd prefer this not to be my epitaph. I take a few deep breaths and within a few minutes my heartbeat has returned to normal and my thoughts are back to something closer to sanity. Or as close as I ever get.

My usual train of thought when contemplating the likely narrative thread of my life is more along the lines of, whatever goes around comes around. That's what they say isn't it? I guess that sometimes it does and sometimes it doesn't. If you're Hitler or Mussolini, then maybe. Is having to shoot your new bride and then commit suicide in a bunker while your hopes and dreams are being bombed to smithereens above your head, appropriate retribution for murdering six million people? Or is being shot by your own people and suspended upside down from a lamp-post appropriate karma for whatever was the worst thing the Italian dictator did? But then there's Stalin who was probably responsible for more deaths than Hitler and seems to have died in his bed. Or Pol Pot from Cambodia who may have killed a higher proportion of his people than anyone else in history and went on to live to a ripe old age. Maybe all four are roasting on a spit in hell and being prodded by demons with red-hot tridents. Let's hope so.

Then there's karma of the Jonathan Aitken, Jeffrey Archer, Harvey Weinstein, Prince Andrew, Boris Johnson variety. It's a wide group who come under the general heading of believing that the rules which apply to everyone else don't apply to them, and who get away with it for years but eventually get a kind of public comeuppance. Dare we allow ourselves just a wisp of schadenfreude when that happens? It's an ugly trait and something I try hard to keep out of my life, but just occasionally one can falter.

Anyway we don't need to get too muddled up in that. The question is whether your good or bad deeds come back to revisit you in this lifetime, or possibly the next. It's a question asked by clerics and philosophers since thinking began, and one I've had cause to ask myself many times in the last four decades or so. Specifically since as a young and foolish man I left my first wife, thereby breaking her heart, and causing my former mother-in-law to wish me harm. I know this because the God-fearing woman summoned me to what at the time was presumed to be her deathbed, and begged my forgiveness for having done so. It was an easy request to acquiesce to because it never occurred to me that her curse would have any efficacy in the real world. I wouldn't have been so easy-going had I known then that just three years later, my second wife and I would have a daughter who was diagnosed with cystic fibrosis, and then required intensive medical treatment for the entirety of her short life, and who died in my arms aged just fourteen.

Thirty years after that I left my second wife, thereby breaking her heart. Despite that, she was and is a wonderful woman, and I think it unlikely that she positively wished me harm. Those close to her may have been less generous. Only a short while after our divorce, however, my new partner walked into her twenty-two year old son's flat one day to find him lying dead on the floor. No sign of anything untoward and not a mark on him: he'd died of an arrhythmia, simply his heart stopped beating shortly after strenuous exercise.

Whatever goes around comes around? Stupid to link these events? After all, it's not all about me. Surely no deity or force of karma would inflict a death sentence on two innocents just to teach me a lesson in pain and suffering. It's egocentric even to think so, but how can we ever know? One can't help thinking "why did this happen to me?" when of course it didn't happen to me. In both cases it happened to two people who most definitely didn't deserve it. I am mere collateral damage.

All very grim and ghastly stuff, and over the years many people have sympathised and meant it kindly when they've said, "I don't know how you survive something like that." And I want to answer that of course you survive it. What other choice do you have? You could curl up in a corner and weep until you can weep no longer, and then fade, waste away and die yourself, and of course there are many times when you feel like doing exactly that. Many times over months and years and, in my case, decades. But however much you feel despair and anger and injustice and outrage; however much you feel grief at what you've missed out on and what they've missed out on, in the end you have to go on. If only because there are people around you who need you to go on. You go on because not going on isn't really an option, unless you genuinely have absolutely nothing to go on for. I've known a few people like that, and they haven't gone on. They got off, and who can blame them?

Anyway I've gone on. I have a surviving daughter, and a surviving stepson, and a wife I love deeply, and so I have lots of reasons to go on. There isn't a day, scarcely even an hour, when I don't think about Sammy or Toby, but you have to go on.

It's just four years since our son Toby died, and his mother and I often talk about how lucky we are. Not of course lucky in comparison to the many people we know who have a houseful of lovely, smart, enterprising, handsome and healthy kids who seem to be a constant source of pride and pleasure to their parents. But fortunate in contrast to the millions upon millions of people around the world, today and in the past, who've undergone tragedy and privation to a level far beyond our worst nightmares. "It's the worst thing that can happen to you – the death of a child." Whenever I've heard that, which is often, I usually shrug and make a half-smile of appreciation for their kind attempt at empathy, but what I'm thinking is, "no it isn't." What is the worst thing? I think the worst thing must be when your child goes missing and you have no idea what happened. That must be the worst thing. In those circumstances, nothing in the world could prevent you from imagining every kind of horror being inflicted on them. Not knowing whether they were alive or dead. If alive, what kind of torture might they be undergoing right at this moment while I am sitting here absolutely powerless to prevent it? If dead, then how and where and why? Beyond imagining though it has been, both of my dead children died in circumstances I know about, neither of them in pain, neither of them feeling lost or unloved. Small comfort, but some comfort nonetheless.

I'll return later to the circumstances of the life and death of both Sammy and Toby, but first of all I'm going back a bit further.

It was on 14 October 1974, at aged 23, that I turned up at the BBC for the first day of what has turned into my fifty-year career in broadcasting. Five years at the Beeb, twenty-five in ITV and twenty more and counting as an independent producer. I've done a lot of jobs in that half a century, from sub-editor to reporter, from producer to chief executive of ITV. I've met or interviewed every British prime minister from Harold Wilson to David Cameron, two American presidents, the prime ministers of Israel and Australia and even Hank

Marvin of The Shadows. I chatted to the Queen at the Royal Variety Performance and to Ella Fitzgerald as she went on stage at Ayresome Park. I swapped caps with Harry Belafonte at the Hay Festival. I've made Joan Bakewell laugh and Joan Rivers cry. I've travelled to some of the most interesting and sometimes dangerous places in the world and I've produced a range of programmes from World in Action to Grumpy Old Men, from a drama-doc about the Westland Affair to Three Men in a Boat, from the Alastair Campbell Diaries to Portrait Artist of the Year. Someone told me at an early stage in my career that it would all be fun, and if it wasn't fun, it would be interesting. Most of it was fun and interesting. Some of it was just fun. Some of it was just interesting. And I always tell people that I never worked for a tyrannical employer until the day I started working for myself.

Fifty years, during which the industry I joined continues to fulfil its role as by far the most popular source of entertainment and information for the majority of the nation, but in the same period more or less everything that happens behind the screens has changed almost beyond recognition. Some of the change has been for the better; for example that nowadays television draws its personnel from a far wider pool of talent than ever was the case when I joined. Some of it is far worse; including the gradual but relentless undermining of the BBC and the withdrawal of the necessary resources for proper investigative journalism on any channel.

My experience in the world of broadcasting is by no means unique; many of the people who joined with me are still around and have their stories and perspectives. But I've been very lucky to be close to the action, either directly in the fray myself or with a privileged ringside seat. So, fifty years in seems like a good moment to write about some of the fun and interesting bits, and also some personal stuff too.

The one thing that all my various roles have involved, directly or indirectly, is storytelling. Hence the name of our TV production company and the name of our website. Storyvault – it's a safe place to keep and tell all your stories. (Or at least I hope it's safe – there may be one or two people in the following narrative who'll feel the need to punch me.)

IN THE BEGINNING ...

———

For the first twelve years my brother and I shared a small bedroom in a small flat on the middle floor of a small three-storey block of council flats in West Norwood. It's difficult to gauge the real size of anything when you're young because you're viewing the world from a height of three or four feet and so things seem bigger than they are. However I've been back since, and can confirm that it was a tiny space in which to try to bring up two boisterous boys. No wonder our parents were constantly under stress and at each other's throats. The scars from frequent noisy rows followed by silence lasting days or weeks have remained with me into adult life, so that I've never been able to tolerate raised voices or domestic acrimony. My instinct on the rare occasions when I'm faced with conflict at work or at home is to flee or fight. I usually manage to get things back into perspective ten minutes or ten hours later, but that's still not a great way to run a railroad.

Dad had been orphaned aged just fourteen and had fended for himself until he was old enough to join the army. He was a "Red Devil" paratrooper in the World War Two, had scars from bullet wounds in both his legs, and crude blotchy tattoos on both arms. Hence I never saw him wear a short-sleeved shirt in his entire life. He stayed in the army for a while and was sent as part of the British responsibility for enforcing the United Nations Mandate in Palestine. He kept a small box of memorabilia which included leaflets branded with the Star of David and exhorting the occupying British soldiers to go home. The polite encouragement had been reinforced by more persuasive methods when the then terrorists (later senior politicians and prime ministers) blew up the King David hotel in Jerusalem killing ninety-one innocents.

Emerging from the war with only an HGV license and no other qualification, Dad managed to get a job as an agent for the London and Manchester Insurance Company. His task was to go door to door around the streets of Herne Hill, Tulse Hill and Brixton, collecting one-and-sixpence here and two bob there, which were the weekly premiums people paid for their life insurance. I think our mum must have stayed at home when we were tiny, but as soon as we were old enough to do as we were told, she got a job selling tickets from the box office in the local Regal cinema. The upside was that we were regular attendees at Saturday morning pictures, which regularly featured Roy Rogers and his equally famous horse Trigger, or the Lone Ranger and his trusty pal Tonto. At the end of a matinee or evening screening, the entire audience would stand to attention for the duration of God Save the Queen. No-one moved until it was finished. I know. Amazing.

These were very different days, when children were expected to fall in with the lives of their parents, and not the other way around as now. We'd walk home from primary school, let ourselves in using a key which hung from a piece of string and was accessible by inserting small fingers through the letter-box, help ourselves to a glass of milk and then sit on the wall outside until someone came home from work.

Aside from my visceral aversion to conflict, the other relevant take out from childhood has been a lifelong fear of poverty. Over the years I've tried to identify whether this was the result of a general awareness of shortages; dressing in clothes which remained in service long after they had worn out, shortages of everything long after wartime rationing had ended. Struggling to recall specifics, I scoured the deepest recesses in my memory bank, eventually to alight on a particular incident which I have come to believe was the cause of my allergy to inertia. It must have taken place on a Friday evening because that was the regular visiting time of the man sent by the council to collect our weekly rent. My recollection is of our mother adopting a demeanour which we didn't often experience, but which left us in no doubt that there was to be no messing about. Having impressed upon us the earnestness of her intentions, she admonished us to be deathly quiet so that anyone knocking on the door would think there was no-one at home. Though she spared us the necessity of spelling it out quite so clearly, the simple fact was that the rent-collector was about to call and we didn't have money to pay. The weekly rent was £5. I believe it was at that moment I resolved that I would never allow myself to be in a similar situation. I started finding ways to earn money at the very first opportunity to do so, and I'm very lucky to be able to say that I've never been out of work from that day to this.

So whatever else might be said about our shortcomings, my brother Steve and I were industrious from the very first opportunity. We had morning paper-rounds from the first time we could ride bikes, we helped the milkman on a Saturday, we had a car-cleaning round in which we arrived at your house with our buckets, sponges and chamois leathers, charging five shillings (25p) for a wash and dry, and ten shillings for a wash, dry and wax polish. Our hands were always chapped and freezing, but at the end of a busy day we'd treat ourselves to a bag of chips and scrunchings (left-over batter) from the local chippy. We always had a bit of pocket money.

My brother was first to take the 11+, the significance of which was little understood at the time, except that we knew it was some kind of turning point. He passed and went to The Strand Grammar School for Boys. I followed him two years later and proceeded to wear his hand-me-down school uniform and P.E. kits, just as I had always worn his other hand-me-down garments.

Just a little way along the road from our school was Tulse Hill Comprehensive, which was the place we would have been doomed to attend had we failed the 11+. The school seemed to be ten times larger than ours and accommodated boys who were very different from us grammar school softies. You didn't want to be caught by any of them while out in the street, alone or with only one friend. In their eyes we were "toffs" or "poofs", and gangs of Tulse Hill kids would knock off and steal caps at minimum, and inflict serious bodily harm at maximum. There had been known to be stabbings.

At that time I was a member of the Boys' Brigade, which was the sort of paramilitary wing of the Methodist church, where we were supposed to attend on Sunday mornings. More importantly however, on Friday evenings we would gather in the local church hall wearing our school uniforms, which were made serious by the addition of a natty white canvas sash stretching diagonally across our bodies, and a smart brown leather belt fastened outside of the jacket by a highly polished brass buckle. Our flannel trousers had to be neatly pressed, our sashes and the white piping on our caps had to be gleaming, and our shoes needed to reflect the overhead strip lighting. A group of about twenty of us would parade around the hall, following shouted orders and marching in step, and our troop featured a brass band in which I played the bugle. Badly. All good fun as far as it went, but the main purpose from my point of view was to play snooker and table-tennis and hang out with my mates. We were parading in that church hall on 22nd November 1963 (coincidentally exactly sixty years ago as I write) when news filtered through that the President of the United States John F. Kennedy had been shot and killed in Dallas, Texas. I was twelve years old at the time and didn't fully understand the significance, but what I did know was that all the grown-ups around us were instantly bloody terrified. They all did their best to act normally, but you could see the anxious glances exchanged between them when they thought we weren't looking. Coming so soon after the Cuban missile crisis just a year before, we kids felt we were growing up in a precarious world. The group leader seemed in much more than averagely earnest when he beseeched God to bestow wisdom on world leaders, but the fact that he had gone as white as a sheet didn't fill us with much confidence that He would comply.

In 1964 the family moved to a modest three bedroomed house in a quiet cul-de-sac in Beckenham, just outside the London boundary. For me this meant a move to the county grammar school, which had higher standards of teaching and offered better opportunities. This proved to be a fork in the road, and one which no doubt propelled me onto a route which was quite different from the one I might otherwise have taken. Whereas most boys at The Strand left school at aged 16 after their O levels and started looking for a job, most boys at Beckenham Grammar school stayed on to take A levels, and some even applied to university. Over the following years, my association with teachers who were able to teach rather than just keep order, and with kids who wanted to learn rather than survive long enough to start earning money, had a profound effect on every aspect of my young life.

One of my good friends over several decades has been the writer and broadcaster Melvyn Bragg whose many accomplishments include having produced and presented hundreds of episodes of The South Bank Show. The format of the programme for those who may not know it was to profile a single individual who has achieved something remarkable in one of the Arts. I remember asking Melvyn if he had been able to identify any common feature among all the geniuses he had met and interviewed. He thought for a moment and then said, "there was this one teacher." And don't we all know it? It was always the teacher of your favourite subject who made it the one you were likely to excel at. In my case it was Keith Potton, who used to pace up and down the aisles between our desks and spit out the speeches from whichever Shakespeare play we were studying with a fearful animation and passion which couldn't fail to impress. It was Mr Potton who pointed out to me that whatever I went on to do in life, wherever I went and whatever range of experiences I had, I could never be everywhere or do everything. So that reading about those times and places, through the words of brilliant writers who had experienced them, was the next best thing you could do. With that piece of advice, I "got it" and have had one, two or three books on the go constantly from that day to this. What a gift. "We read so we can know that we're not alone."

I still felt a continuing need to earn as much money as I could, and so I got a Saturday job in the local greengrocer's shop round the corner in Elmer's End high street. The shop was owned by George who was an affable Greek, but the guy who did all the running was called Frank and was the original "Jack the lad". Frank was having some sort of relationship with George's sister Irene and they lived together in a flat over the shop. I was sixteen and keen to get stuck in, so Frank offered to take me with him up to the fruit and vegetable market where he'd buy that day's fresh produce. I'd get out of bed at 4am, report for work at 4.20, and we'd be off in his battered old white transit van to see what was what. Everyone working in the market seemed to be related, or at least to be on remarkably familiar terms. Deals were done swiftly through an indecipherable code, and after half an hour or so I'd be loading up ten boxes of tomatoes, wooden trays of cucumber and celery, sacks of raw beetroot, cabbage, kale, cauliflower, and whatever fruit was in season. We'd load the van until the suspension was groaning, and then dash back through the gradually filling streets of the suburbs to Elmer's End where we'd be in a hurry to get our produce out on display on the pavement at the front of the shop.

On one side of the shop was a baker where they baked their own bread and rolls, and on the other side was an old-fashioned butcher, so that our daily reward for hard labour in the small hours of the morning was to fry up an implausible quantity of the best bacon from next door until it was crispy, mix in as many as we wanted of the tomatoes we'd just bought from the market, and squeeze the concoction into a warm roll fresh from the oven. Wolfed down after being awake and working for four hours on a winter's morning, these were the best and most delicious breakfasts I've ever eaten before or since.

It was an education. Most of our customers were young mums from the area who would drop off their kids and then come along to do their shopping. There were two greengrocers' shops within a short space on the street, and ours was instantly and noticeably the most popular, which George put down to the freshness of the fruit and vegetables, and Frank put down to the freshness of his humour. His mouth ran away with a constant commentary as the queues formed, and there was absolutely no double-entendre or cliché too distasteful to be included in his repartee.

Anyone asking Frank for a cucumber was obviously asking for trouble, and he would duly oblige by picking up an elongated monster, pressing it to his groin as he approached the customer, yelling "I can't get it all in," as he tried to squeeze it into their shopping bags. "Oh my goodness, isn't he terrible?" was the usual response, and possibly a little frisson of flirtation counted as a high spot in an otherwise uneventful day. Two large cabbages would be stuffed under his pullover in a grim parody of over-large bosoms, and bananas were naturally a source of endless schoolboy humour. No innuendo was spared and nothing was safe or sacred. I feel I must have been a bit sheltered because even in those pre-enlightenment days I was continually astonished that these entirely respectable women didn't slap his face or otherwise take him to task. Business was booming.

For me, with my ever-ready radar for possibilities, the situation created continuous opportunities of what we might tactfully call the "Mrs Robinson" variety, and one day an attractive woman twice my age let me know that her husband was working away from home and that she would welcome a visit. I was transfixed; part excited and part terrified, but all things taken into account, I was ready to acquiesce. Before I finally made up my mind however, I confided my intention to George.

"I wouldn't do that if I were you," he said.

I was dismayed. "Why not?"

"Because if you do, you'll put yourself in a position where some other bloke you've never met may well come along and kill you, and you'll know that he's absolutely justified in doing so."

Oh. I hadn't looked at it like that. Dammit. George was probably right. I was desperately keen to say yes, but decided I should say no. It was an early and rare example of me making the sensible decision in such matters.

I don't recall anyone asking me the question, but if they had I probably would have said that when I grew up I wanted to be a journalist, just because I was interested in the news and English was the only thing I was any good at. I didn't watch much telly at the time, but I know for sure that I was aware of the World in Action series. It was an investigative current affairs show on ITV on a Monday evening, and was a "must watch" in our household. The title sequence involved dramatic music and an animation of Leonardo's Vitruvian man, all of which sent the pulse racing even before the programme got underway. They'd be on the trail of former Nazi war criminals who'd fled to South America, or guilty capitalists who'd stolen the life savings of hapless clients. From an early age, the idea of "righting wrongs" and the baddies getting their just deserts appealed to me; I can't honestly identify a moment, but this may have been the time when the seeds were sewn.

Among the sounds we were listening to were protest songs by performers with appealing names like Country Joe and the Fish, or Arlo Guthrie. Many of their songs had something directly or indirectly to do with the war in Vietnam, which we didn't really understand the reasons for but just knew that we were generally against. Not least because a lot of Americans not much older than us seemed to be going home with no limbs or in body-bags. That's not to mention the impact of napalm or Agent Orange on the long-suffering Vietnamese.

In March 1968, my friend Nita and I found ourselves among thousands of others who looked and sounded much like us, marching towards the US Embassy in Grosvenor Square. We were carrying banners with slogans urging the Americans to get out of Vietnam, and chanting "Hey, hey LBJ, how many children have you killed today?" as well as a mesmerising call-and-response along the lines of "What do we want? Peace! Where do we want it? Vietnam! When do we want it? Now!"

I recall police mounted on horseback starting to become restive, and when someone set fire to a Stars and Stripes, all hell broke loose. Demonstrators were climbing over fences leading into the Square, and truncheon-wielding officers were charging and belabouring long-haired student-types about the head and neck. It was all very ugly and out of hand, and I was excited and terrified at the same time, a mix you could easily see becoming addictive.

We were positioned on the road to one side of the Embassy, and Nita took it into her head that she wanted to scrawl some abusive slogan in lipstick onto the glass doors at the side of the building. We had just about plucked up enough courage to do so and were ready to advance when a phalanx of police on foot suddenly appeared in front of us. There was the sound of rolling thunder, and I looked up to see a posse of mounted police galloping in our direction, apparently quite out of control. I learned later that someone had thrown glass marbles onto the ground in front of them, and the whole thing was bloody awful. Nonetheless the adrenalin ran high that day, and we all ended up at home, unharmed but exhilarated by the certain knowledge that we had done some good in the world. As if.

I must have been aware that other kids in the class were applying to university, but the idea didn't initially appear on my horizon, and I guess the assumption was that I would leave school at eighteen and look for a job. A number of my friends had offers of places, conditional on the results of their A levels. I think it's fair to say that my teachers were surprised when I did better than most of my classmates in the exams. These were well before the days when everyone excelled at everything, and my two Bs and a D grades put me right up there with people who could definitely get a place at university if they wished. It was too late for the start of the next term, but suddenly there was a fork coming up in the road ahead of me and I had a big decision to make.

It's important to be fair to the memory of my mum and dad, and I'm struggling to distil and express the view they took about what should happen next. They had been prevented by WW2 from having much more than elementary education, and our dad was very much of the "get out there and start earning your living" persuasion. Mum always had aspirations that we should shimmy up the class–ladder, and there's no doubt that she wanted whatever was best for her sons. But this was unknown territory, the kind of thing that happens to posh people. Certainly no-one from our extended family had ever even considered going to university, so the whole thing was a strange and mysterious prospect. I think we agreed that I'd apply and see what happened. In the meantime I'd get a job to save some money which would help if I did end up continuing my education. In those days you could get a means-tested grant from the local council towards your fees, but you had to pay your own subsistence. My parents looked ready to help with that, but I was in no doubt that I'd have to be making an effort and a contribution.

I was always going to major in English, but where to do so? Some people take into account the reputation of the university, the details of the course, or whether any of their schoolmates are also going to a particular place. My analysis was based on what I took to be the likelihood that I'd spend most if not all of my working life in London and the south of England, so this was an opportunity to get as far away as possible, and learn something about some distant part of the country. So I looked at the map and my top three choices were Newcastle upon Tyne, Lancaster and Belfast.

My mother wasn't thrilled by any of these prospects, but she had a particular and understandable apprehension that I might go to Belfast, not least because this was 1969 and The Troubles were ripping the province apart. We were all excited when I was called for an interview at Lancaster, but suddenly none of us had the slightest idea what you might be expected to wear for such an occasion. Something casual? The only clothes I owned other than my old school uniform were jeans and T-shirts with pictures of Che Guevara or Frank Zappa on the front, and they were certainly not suitable. Something smart? I didn't own a suit, and had neither the money nor the inclination to buy one. In the end I was togged up in an ill-fitting grey flannel suit belonging to my dad, and I couldn't have felt less comfortable if I'd been dressed as an astronaut.

It was snowing heavily when I came out of the railway station and asked a taxi-driver to take me to Lancaster University. It came as a surprise that the place was a campus built some distance out of town, and when the driver dropped me off in an underpass, I found myself amidst a maze of concrete walls and couldn't find anything resembling an entrance. Snow was now falling copiously in heavy globs, my suit didn't fit, and I felt as if I'd suddenly landed ill-prepared in a strange and mysterious land in which I knew nothing and no-one.

For some reason best known to myself, I'd ended up applying to do a joint honours in English and Philosophy, and of course it quickly transpired in my interview that I didn't actually know what Philosophy was. I must have just liked the sound of it. English and Philosophy; it would have sounded so cool at the time when asked the question at parties. The interviewing academics were far more patient and tolerant than I would have been, but nonetheless I left the room feeling humiliated and twenty thousand leagues out of my depth. Now back in and amongst what seemed to me to be the brutalist architecture, I had no idea how I was going to find my way to the railway station, and there was no indication of where and how one could catch a bus. So I set off to walk, in the snow, which was getting deeper and deeper and was now way past my ankles. Even now I don't know how far it was, but it quickly became more and more obvious that I had made a silly mistake. By the time I eventually reached the station I was freezing cold, wet, hungry, bedraggled, and about as depressed as I'd ever been.

I arrived back in London after what felt like six months later, then caught the suburban train, then walked some more. My poor mother had been waiting anxiously all day to hear news and was actually standing at the front door to greet me when I eventually slogged up the garden path. She must have seen the anguished expression on my face from yards away.

"How did it go?" she asked.

"I don't want to talk about it," I replied, stomped up the stairs, slammed by bedroom door, threw myself on my bed and slept in my father's suit. What a total, self-centred, selfish inconsiderate little sod I must have been. My mum had spent the entire time since I'd left fourteen or more hours earlier being worried sick and rooting for her youngest son, and all I could say was "I don't want to talk about it." She and I remembered and laughed about it many years later, but even if she forgave me, I never forgave myself.

Amazingly I was offered a place in Lancaster, but by that time I'd had what turned out to be a far more agreeable visit to the university in Newcastle, which had what I considered to be the advantage of being situated within the city. While I didn't know much, I did know enough to realise that it would be a far more rewarding experience to live among real people rather than in an artificial bubble of students.

The course was English Language and Literature, and included a lot of Linguistics and Anglo-Saxon, which I didn't feel all that thrilled about because it sounded a bit more like actual work than merely reading enjoyable books.

It's not easy to convey quite what a thing it was that a member of our family was going to university. This was way before universities and polytechnics were merged, and at that time maybe four in a hundred schoolchildren went on to study for a degree. University was for very posh and very clever people, and none of us had ever hitherto been thought to fall into either category. Nonetheless the deal was done and I had a year to fill, during which I had to earn enough money to realistically subsidize my living expenses in my first year as an undergraduate.

"'Undergraduate!' Will you listen to it? He's going to be a toff now."

GAP YEAR

The mists of unreliable memory are now obscuring the sequence of events which led me to apply for a job as a porter in St Christopher's Hospice in Sydenham. The idea of an institution dedicated to easing the passage of the dying was a completely new one at the time. A remarkable woman called Dame Cicely Saunders had pioneered the idea, and I believe this was the first of its kind in the country.

Before the opening of St Christopher's, most facilities for the terminally ill had been side wards of the "abandon hope all ye who enter" variety, shunting patients away from the main work of the hospital as an expression of the failure of modern medicine to cure and restore them. People came to St Christopher's when they were deemed to have six weeks or less to live, and while no further effort was going to be made to cure them of whatever had brought them to this state, every effort was going to be made to ensure that their final days would be as peaceful and pain-free as possible. While doctors seeking to cure a patient might hold back on prescribing analgesics which may not otherwise improve the medical condition, now there was no reason for such restraint. The idea was to situate these poor unfortunate people in the last days of their lives in a bright, airy environment, surrounded by well-kept gardens, and to do whatever was necessary to balance their pain with their awareness of the day. St Christopher guiding them gently over their final journey. Such was their relief from suffering that some of them actually rallied for a period, but at that point in history it was never going to be for long.

So at this time I'm eighteen years old, totally naïve and unworldly, reporting for work, and I'm going to be thrust instantly among the terminally ill, helping to move them about in their beds and wheelchairs, and subject daily and hourly to sights and sounds for which I was, to say the least of it, unprepared.

My job involved long hours and shiftwork from the very beginning, and I was made familiar with the switchboard and reception desk which I would be manning whenever the permanent operator was at lunch or otherwise off-duty. All calls coming into the hospice were fielded at the front desk, and for some unaccountable reason I developed a sort of whispered "Hello St Christopher's" when I answered. Possibly I thought this in some way conveyed compassion. These were days long before anything of the "how may I re-direct your call" variety, and I'd be required to say, "hold on a moment, I'll put you through," and take the appropriate jack-plug and insert it into the relevant input connecting the caller to the ward.

It hardly needs saying that dying and death was all around us. That was the point, but it was all very new territory for me and I was into a fast learning curve. I discovered quickly, for example, that medical teams can usually tell when someone in their care has reached the last few hours of their life. This consists of a distinctive type of shallow breathing, sometimes colloquially known as the death rattle. At that point it would be necessary to contact the nearest and dearest, and to ask them to come into the hospice as quickly as possible. Quite often I'd be required to make that call, and of course simply to do so was enough to alert the next of kin that their loved one was slipping away. It would be anything between a few minutes and a few hours before you'd see a car speeding through the entrance gates and screeching to a halt outside, and one or more distraught people hurrying into the reception area and rushing towards the stairs or lifts. On some occasions they were too late, and in such cases the ward sister would call me and ask me to identify and delay the dead person's relatives in the foyer, for fear of them blundering into their room at an inopportune moment. On such occasions I'd never take my eyes off the car park and front door, just in case I might miss or mis-identify the relevant people. It's not surprising that when I'd stop someone and ask if they were here to see "Mrs Jones" and then ask them to wait a moment while I summoned the ward sister to come down to see them, they instantly knew what I was telling them and would collapse in a heap of tears and distress. This happened on maybe three or four occasions in a few weeks, and I can't help thinking that it was an inappropriate responsibility to place on the shoulders of an eighteen-year-old know-nothing such as myself.

I have an idea that at that time probably two or three of the patients at St Christopher's were dying each week, and I'm sure it must have been explained to me very early that part of my duties would be to attend in the mortuary when the undertakers would come to collect their bodies.

This situation arose for the first time only a day or so after I'd started work at the hospice.

A slightly more senior and experienced porter was on duty with me, still showing me around, when two undertakers arrived to collect a woman who had died the previous day. I think the other chap was about twenty-five and we'll call him Jack. No doubt Jack meant well, or possibly he wanted to be able to share this aspect of the job as quickly as possible, so he suggested that I come down to witness the process before managing it myself next time. Was I okay with that? Yes of course I was. I was a pretending to be a grown up.

The two undertakers, Jack and I went downstairs to the mortuary, which consisted of a room with two banks of refrigerators, each of which had a series of little doors stacked one upon the other. A lined ledger on a side table contained a list of the names of the occupant of each compartment. On this occasion Jack consulted the book and ascertained that our patient was in number eight, which was on the third level, at about shoulder height for me. It's fifty-five years since all this happened but I can, as the saying goes, remember it as though it was yesterday. What seemed like quite a flimsy wooden coffin was laid on the floor a short distance away from the fridges. The door was opened and Jack grabbed the corner of a sliding tray and pulled it out. This was my first ever sight of a dead body, and it was a shocking thing to experience. Even though the woman was wearing a thin nightdress, one could see without doubt that she was skeletally thin. Her skin was yellow and jaundiced, she had a few strands of wispy white hair, and her face was contorted in an expression which did not, I'm sorry to say, indicate a peaceful departure.

Mercifully I had only a few seconds to take all this in because the sliding tray was instantly lifted onto the floor next to the coffin. Jack took one hand, the two undertakers took the other hand and her feet, and her featherweight body was lifted up and placed in the coffin. A lid was placed on top, the body signed for in the ledger, and the whole process was over. A final journey for the unfortunate soul, and a life-long and traumatic memory for me.

Over the following few weeks, I performed a similar service for dead people many times. Obviously I never got used to it, but of course it became just a bit easier as time went by.

During occasional breaks I'd chat to the nurses, and inevitably we'd get onto the subject of their morale and motivation for work-ing at St Christopher's. "If you work in a normal hospital," I'd say, "patients will come in after a car crash, all bashed to pieces and in a terrible state, but at least you get the satisfaction of seeing them walk out as good as new in a few weeks' time. But no-one ever walks out of here feeling mended or better." "No," they'd reply, "but our patients are embarking on the most important journey of their lives, and if we can help them to get through it with as little pain and distress as possible, that's reward enough." Wow. How could you ever find words to express sufficient admiration?

Even something so grim had its lighter moments, and I remember that one of my less distressing duties was to take delivery of the morning newspapers, place them on a trolley and walk round the wards, selling copies to anyone who was well enough and still sufficiently engaged with the world they were shortly to be leaving. Inspired by the example of the wonderful nurses, I'd always do my best to be cheerful and chatty with patients, and I got to know a few of them. I was going to use the expression "to pass the time of day" but somehow that seems wildly inappropriate. Anyway there was this one chap called Jacob who hadn't spoken to anyone at all since he'd been admitted to the hospice several weeks earlier. I think I must have learned from Jack or one of the nurses that Jacob liked to have a copy of the Daily Mirror, and that he kept some loose change in the top drawer of his side table. I'd chat to him while I was sorting out the money, and one day I didn't have the necessary change so I took a ten shilling note and told him that I'd repay him on the following morning. Remember that Jacob hadn't uttered a word to anyone all the time he'd been a patient here, and everyone assumed he never would.

Next day I was doing the rounds, selling the newspapers, and when I got to Jacob I placed his copy of the newspaper on his side table and rifled in his drawer for the purchase price. I completed the transaction and was just about to go to the next bed when I heard someone say, "Stuart". I looked around in amazement, as did one of the nurses who happened to be alongside, and we both heard Jacob say, "you owe me five bob."

I'm not sure now if I was running away from the hospice or running towards a new opportunity in which I could get someone to pay me a decent amount of money without doing any actual work. One way or the other, I got myself a job as an assistant in the Lewisham public library service. I think I'd persuaded myself that this would give me plenty of opportunity to hide amongst dusty archives and spend my time filling in a few of the yawning gaps in my literary knowledge. That wasn't quite how it worked. In fact it turned into an early lesson in the way that some organisations which appear to be entirely bland and innocuous, can in actual fact be a crucible of vicious rivalries and petty politics.

In this case the issue at the core of everything was the amazingly strict and structured class system which had humble Library Assistants such as myself right at the bottom where we no doubt belonged, and the Town Clerk right at the top where he no doubt also properly belonged. In the middle was a Kafkaesque hierarchy in which so-called professional librarians, (people who had been to Library School and studied the Dewey decimal classification system,) went to great lengths to assert and maintain their superiority over the former, and did everything they possibly could to ingratiate themselves with the latter.

No measure was deemed to be too petty in the quest by the professionals to sustain the distinction between themselves and us mere factotums. We, for example, were permitted to man ("man" was okay in those days; these days I assume we must say "person") the front desk. It was okay for us to use a natty but decidedly analogue date stamp to indicate the "return by" deadline on a sticker inside the front cover, and to receive returned books and exchange them for the reader's library ticket. Even this was done under the watchful eyes of whichever professional was assigned to the Enquiry Desk which was situated just a few feet in front of us on Reception. However even this apparently simple transaction was not without its complications.

When one reader asked me where he could find the fiction section, I pointed to the two outside walls where novels where shelved, A-L by author on this wall, M-Z on the other. The reader headed off happily, only to be intercepted a few moments later by the professional librarian on duty, Mr Scrimple, asking, "was there something I can help you with?" "No," said the reader, "the young man has already told me what I needed to know."

Scrimple grimaced and then made an instant beeline for me. "Never ever," he told me, "give information to a reader again. That's what we are for." I'd wondered. Later that afternoon a member of the public approached my desk and asked if I could tell her the time. "I'm sorry," I said, "I'm afraid you'll have to ask that gentleman at the Enquiry Desk." It wasn't going well.

A further example related to the system of fines which the library ran in order to deter people from keeping books beyond their return date. I can't remember how much people had to pay, but let's say it was two shillings per week overdue. Quite quickly after I started the job, I noticed that any reader who came back with a few overdue books and was therefore required to pay a fine which might by then have amounted to ten shillings or more, almost invariably walked straight out of the library without choosing any other books. This seemed to me instantly to defeat the obvious and fundamental purpose of the library, which was to encourage people to borrow books and to read them. I therefore instituted my own personal system in which I made a snap assessment of whether the person concerned could easily afford to pay the fine, and if I deemed that they couldn't, I'd whisper that there was nothing to pay on this occasion and direct them towards the bookshelves. I quickly found that my theory that this leniency would lead directly to increased readership was borne out by the empirical evidence.

I think you may have guessed what's coming. Yes that's right; someone grassed me up, and soon the unfeasibly long and slender deputy chief librarian called Mr Scrotum confronted me. He had gathered evidence over several days, he told me, and had chapter and verse of my various transgressions. Apparently I had committed a very serious misdemeanour, and there was even a moment where I thought I might be obliged to cover the money lost from uncollected fines from my wages. I was left in no doubt that I was never to do it again. I did.

Having said that we didn't appear to mind alienating our readers by imposing fines that they could ill-afford, it was still the case that the worst thing that could possibly happen was for a reader to make a complaint about the library service or, even worse, about any individual named librarian, to the Town Clerk. It mattered not whether a complaint was justifiable or justified; merely the fact that it was made was sufficient to provoke terror in the heart of the librarian. This in turn gave rise to a degree of sycophancy when faced with the most unreasonable complaints which turned my stomach.

The only exception to this rule involved the Branch Librarian in Deptford, Mr Spine, who happened to be a close friend of the Town Clerk, and indeed even lived close by and regularly played golf with him. One evening Mr Spine and I were the only two people on duty. I was manning the desk and he was somewhere in the background studying the Racing Post when a ferocious looking woman came in and placed one of our "reminder of overdue books" postcards on the desk.

"I want to speak to whoever sent me this," she said.

"You mean whomever?" (No I didn't say it, but that's what I was thinking.)

Obviously I had no idea who had sent that particular reminder to her, but the identity of the individual seemed irrelevant. I was about to reply that it was me when I sensed Mr Spine at my shoulder.

"It was me, I sent it to you," he said, "what seems to be the problem?"

"The problem, my good man," she said, "is that you are accusing me of having borrowed this book and not having returned it, and I have never borrowed this book and therefore cannot return it."

Mr Spine said nothing, but quietly picked up the postcard and went to our highly sophisticated filing system, and returned a moment later with a little brown cardboard pocket and a little blue cardboard ticket covered in handwritten words. He placed both on the desk.

"Is this your library ticket?" he said. The woman agreed that it was. "Is this the ticket from the book in question?" he said.

"Yes," she could hardly disagree, "but I've already told you that I never borrowed this book."

Mr Spine kept his voice at the same moderate level. "This is your readers' ticket, and this is the book ticket, so there can be no doubt that you have borrowed the book."

I thought the woman would explode. She puffed herself up like a 3D version of one of those frogs you see in David Attenborough shows, and I thought her tongue was about to come out like a projectile yoyo to deliver a poison sting just above his collar-line. In fact she was unable to find the right words, and instead she turned and stormed out of the building.

Mr Spine said nothing further to me, and I was just digesting this unusual situation when the outer door opened once again, and the same woman strode up to the counter. The Librarian faced her squarely.

"Just so I have this clear before I take my complaint to the Town Hall," she said. "Can I just make certain? Are you, sir, calling me a liar?"

Mr Spine did not miss a beat. "Yes," he said. "And not only are you a liar, but you are also a filthy liar, and I want this book back in the library before we close, or we will take measures to force you to pay for it."

You think I'm joking? I'm really not. Those were his words. And guess what happened. Half an hour later, just as I was about to bolt the door, the woman came back to the library, returned the book and paid the fine. "Turns out my son had borrowed it without telling me," she said, and vanished into the night.

The best part of my job was that twice a week, on Tuesday and Thursday afternoons, I was required to man the mobile library. Once again I'm allowed to say "man" because, as you'll see, the job was far too hazardous to be undertaken by a woman without recourse to a pepper-spray or a Smith and Wesson. The mobile library was a huge caravan which would be towed by Land Rover to some far-flung outpost of the borough and left for several hours. Props would be placed under both ends, and a padlock put on the handbrake so that the locals couldn't set it free, thereby allowing it to career down the hill. I'd be left alone for anything between four and six hours to stamp in and stamp out books for people who couldn't or wouldn't go to the main branches.

The majority of the customers were local women who would almost invariably come in to return a maximum of eight romances from the famous publishers of the genre called Mills and Boon. Each volume was covered in a slight variation of the same artwork showing a pretty but usually humble young woman, being apparently propositioned by a remarkably good looking slightly older man, who was in turn all decked out in attire indicating that he was perhaps a foreign prince - quite possibly from a small and little-known but seemly monarchy situated in an unspecified geography somewhere in Eastern Europe or the Levant.

Most often these women would dump the eight books they'd borrowed and instantly scoop up the next eight books from the romance shelves. "But how do you know you haven't read those already?" I'd enquire. "It doesn't matter," they'd say, "they're all exactly the same anyway." And they were. I leafed through a few volumes just to get the gist, and usually Lord Chard had the hots for young Estelle, who was sure she was too humble to be a suitable match for him, but whose poverty in the end could not stand in the way of true love. There was never anything racy or erotic about it all, and certainly no soft porn. These were just nice stories which no doubt provided a much needed escape from the humdrum of life on the estate where the old man might well have been perfectly okay, and indeed might even have been from the Levant, but certainly wasn't Lord Chard.

The mobile library was a rather quiet and forlorn experience for quite a lot of the time, and I'd usually employ the beneficial effects of a couple of cans of Guinness to help to while away the hours before the Land Rover would return to collect me. On one or two occasions, however, the mobile attracted the unwanted attention of groups of the local kids with nothing better to do, and they'd start circling the caravan on their bikes, rather like those old movies of indigenous Indians circling the wagon train, but lobbing large stones and bottles rather than shooting flaming arrows. In those days of course we had no effective mobile communications device for summoning assistance, so all I could do was to close the doors and windows and await the cavalry.

The cavalry which eventually came was in the form of either Paddy or Tommy. Paddy was a delightful Irishman who was always cheerful, and with whom I used to sing "Danny Boy" as a duet on our way back to the branch. The blood vessels in his neck would protrude so alarmingly when we got to the high notes that I feared for his life. Tommy was equally entertaining. He had been a rather senior civil engineer in earlier days, but had sustained a blow to the head in an industrial accident which had entirely wiped out his short-term memory. I was alongside Tommy one day when the branch librarian at Lewisham, Mr Waddington, came up to speak to him. "Oh Tommy, do you remember that I asked you yesterday to take this book ..." He got no further before Tommy interrupted him. "Mr Waddington," he said, "I can't remember what I had for breakfast. I can't remember what anyone said to me five minutes ago. And if I could," he paused, "do you really think I'd be working in this fucking dump?" Mr Waddington nodded sagely. "Fair enough," he said, and moved on.

It was about this time that the first Chinese restaurants started popping up in the suburbs of London, and were something of a curiosity in a world in which a Wimpy Bar was about as cosmopolitan as it got. My mate David and I used to pop into the Chinese a few doors away for a set lunch at what seemed an extraordinarily low price. I want to say three courses for five bob, but can that be possible? So it was that we began to be weaned away from ghastly hot mince pies at lunchtime and introduced to chicken chow mein and sweet and sour pork, which seemed very exotic, but which I later learned were about as authentically Chinese as an Arbroath Smokie.

Just exactly how unworldly and stupid we were was exemplified by my friend Tim's older brother who prided himself on embracing all this new-fangled food, and offered to demonstrate his wide knowledge by taking his entire family out for dinner in the recently opened Chinese round the corner. The family sat down and began to take in the everlasting fountain bathed in multi-coloured lights and to marvel at the woman's arm waving (was it hello or goodbye?) in perpetual motion, while Tim's brother examined the menu and then summoned the waiter. Rather ostentatiously (it was later reported) the family's first-born borrowed a biro from the waiter and began to tick off items on the menu.

"Go to the kitchen and cook this," he said imperiously. The far more sensible waiter paused for a moment to study the form. Eventually he spoke.

"'Nuff food here to feed army," he said.

Not to be gainsaid, Big Brother insisted that he knew what he was doing, and fifteen minutes later a procession of perhaps twenty waiters and waitresses, beginning with the tallest and ending with the tiniest and cutest in pigtails, delivered more food than could have been readily consumed by the Household Cavalry, including horses. Big Brother made the best of it, but had to work hard not to shed a tear when the bill arrived.

Aside from the marginally more cosmopolitan cuisine, the other regular diversion which helped to get me through some otherwise tedious days occurred as a result of the library's proximity to the Registry Office. On maybe half a dozen occasions within a few months, I'd be nursing my pie and pint in the snug bar, only to be approached by a couple asking me if I had a spare twenty minutes to be a witness at their wedding next door. I obliged on every occasion, and happily signed the register and accepted a celebratory drink. Most explained that all their friends and family thought they were already married, and so they were just heading off as a couple to formalise things. On several occasions the couple already shared the same surname before the marriage, which was weird but I didn't ever ask.

It's well known that "The Sixties" didn't really take place in the sixties, and it was only now that it was 1970 that some of the alleged benefits of the era began to arrive in the form of casual sex. I think it must have been the certainty that I was just passing through on my way to university (and therefore unlikely to become a complication) which contributed to any favour I might have found among the female members of the library staff, and several of their friends. In any event, by the time I got around to heading off to the frozen north to begin my varsity experience, the world of work had taught me quite a lot of useful things, and how to do actual work on a regular basis was only one of them.

GOING UP

Looking back on it, I can still scarcely believe that I actually packed a trunk, provided for me by my grandparents from their attic, and sent it on ahead to the Castle Leazes halls of residence on the Town Moor in Newcastle upon Tyne. A few days later I caught the cut-price-for-students' train called The Highwayman, which was discounted because it took what seemed to be about three weeks to get there, travelling via every town and village in England with a vowel in the name.

The temperature when I arrived and alighted from the train was about ten degrees cooler than when I'd left London, and never really warmed up for the next four years. Struggling up Northumberland Street in what I worked out was the general direction of Castle Leazes, I asked a passer-by if I was on the right route for the Town Moor. The poor chap looked confused.

"I divvi na. Y'sl hefta larn yeself the reet root bonny lad." Or something.

Over the next days and weeks I gained all sorts of important insights into life in the land of the Geordie. A "stottie" was a flat loaf which would be filled with ham and pease pudding for a treat; going into the middle of the city was going "doon the toon", a Scotch was beer, Newcastle Brown Ale was an icon, Exhibition wasn't lager, and the Magpies were a religion. Every Saturday, every male aged between eight and eighty from many miles around could be seen heading in the general direction of St James's Park, wearing whatever was the latest variation of the familiar black and white strip, stopping only briefly at every pub along the route. You could tell the progress of the match from any outside vantage point up to three miles away, merely by aggregating the massive waves of oohs and aahs emanating from the vast crowd. Everything about the town, from the turnover in pubs and restaurants to the productivity in the shipyards, was index-linked to the performance of Newcastle United, and I quickly learned that things were seldom going well.

I happily moved into my study-bedroom at Castle Leazes, sorted out my record player, and carefully attached my posters of each of the four Beatles, all decked out in psychedelic garb, to the walls. I also had a poster of the delicious Bridget Bardot, with some pretty flowers only just concealing her breasts, which would never be tolerated today. (That's the poster which wouldn't be tolerated – not the concealment.)

I realised it would be important to get to know and be on good terms with my near neighbours along the corridor to the shared kitchen. I quickly learned that the ever-present slight whiff of rotting flesh coming from the general direction of next door was not, as I at first assumed, the stink of privilege. It was due to the Right Honourable Conroy Ryder's habit of hanging the brace of pheasants he'd bagged on his shooting weekend just outside his window, uncomfortably close to the exterior light. We did a deal which involved me making no complaint in exchange for a share of the weekly feast, and the resulting redistribution of wealth felt like I'd struck a blow for socialism.

Just like me, most of the students knew no-one and were as anxious as I was to meet like-minded people. I was on the lookout for "heads" with whom I might share something in common, characterised by long hair, scruffy flared jeans and T-shirts, and a general demeanour of studied disinterest. I found my tribe pretty quickly;

Keith Marsden, Kath (real name Andrew) Kirby, Sue Jeffs, Lesley
Booth, Gill and Peter. And so the fun began. Peter had brought King
Crimson and I'd brought Ummagumma. Kath had brought Hendrix
and I'd brought Wheels of Fire. All of us had brought a healthy thirst
for knowledge, experience and alcohol.

A high priority for me was to get involved in the student newspaper, and so I took the first opportunity to make myself known in
the offices of The Courier. It was lucky for me that by far the biggest
departments in Newcastle were the Medical School and the School
of Agriculture. Though highly regarded, the English and Politics
departments were relatively small, so I found myself welcomed with
open arms by the existing newspaper team, and before I knew what I
was agreeing to, I had accepted the job and title of News Editor. An
early lesson in the opportunities made available simply by turning up.

The social aspects of university life went well from the very
start, and the new-found freedom which was simply a function of
being away from home was fully used and abused. Loud music, too
much beer and bad behaviour in all the categories you are imagining.
Though I'd acquired a pretty good work ethic during my year in
full time paid employment, I found that I didn't take too well to the
actual study aspect of university life. I'd probably imagined a lot of
reading the Romantic poets while sitting under a shady oak, followed
by profound and learned discussions on the nature of being, extending way into the small hours and lubricated by a cheeky claret. The
reality was more along the lines of having to learn Sir Gawain and
the Green Knight by heart because acquiring the ability to translate
it from the original wasn't a realistic option. I was much more interested in the D.H.Lawrence than I was in Piers Plowman, but that
wasn't the course I'd signed up for. Certainly there were late night
discussions, but they were mostly fuelled by Guinness and weed
rather than anything originating in a grape, and therefore quickly
descended into juvenile speculation of the "will she, might she?"

variety. I regret to say that not much of it was very edifying or felt like a good return to the taxpayer for generously subsidising our education.

Contact with my family at this time consisted of a call once a week on a Sunday afternoon, made from the pay-phone attached to a wall in the foyer, and which was as brief as I could reasonably make it. I'd also receive a newsy letter from Mum most weeks, which I'd tear open because it quite often also contained a five-pound note, which was the hard-earned result of a part-time job she had taken in order to subsidise me. I try not to have too many regrets as I look back on my life, but I'm sorry to say that I experience a genuine sting of remorse whenever I recall what an ungrateful little sod I was in those days. My mum must have worked hard to be able to send me those five pound notes, and I can't honestly remember thanking her properly, if at all. Shame on me. I can only hope that she's been looking down on me from heaven all these years, and knows what a shit I feel and how grateful I am in retrospect.

None of this was made any better by the fact that I did not manage to make it home in that first year, and by the time I walked back up the path at my parents' house in Beckenham, I'd lost more than a stone in weight and hadn't had a haircut for the best part of two years. I knocked on the door, waited for a moment or two, and when my mum appeared, she looked at me without any sign of recognition for three seconds and then burst into tears. The poor woman deserved so much better.

Despite my manifold shortcomings, somehow I managed to get through year one and by year two I had become the editor of the university newspaper, which I found to be both totally absorbing and almost totally time-consuming. The job involved writing something to fill every gap which hadn't been filled by the news editor, the features editor, the sports editor and the provider of the weekly crossword. The name of our features editor escapes me, but I recall that he was drawn to work at the paper when he spotted the crossword clue for a five-letter word was "cardboard fish." I'd also write the weekly editorial, which usually consisted of a naïve rant about the iniquities of the government of the day and the virtues of an egalitarian society. It's instructive to consider in retrospect that we regarded the mild-mannered Prime Minister Ted Heath to be dangerously right wing because he was taking on the might of the trade unions in general, and the miners in particular. Little did we realise that the vast majority of our readers would go on enthusiastically to embrace and perpetuate the capitalist system.

One Sunday I was walking through the university on my way to the Courier office when a small people-carrier pulled up alongside me and the driver asked if I could direct them to the students' union. I pointed out that they we were standing alongside it, but that the union building didn't open on Sundays. How could I help?

"We want to do a concert here tonight." The words were spoken in a distinct Liverpool accent and I looked in the direction of the back seat where Paul McCartney was sitting with his wife Linda and alongside them I recognised the guitarist Denny Lane. It was their new band Wings and they were doing a whistle-stop tour of impromptu concerts, just to get their hand in. Wow. I was thinking quickly.

"The union won't open again until tomorrow, but the hall of residence houses about a thousand students." I suggested that maybe it might be possible to clear one of the dining halls.

"Could you find out if that's okay?" said McCartney. "And can you recommend a decent hotel?"

I always say that this was the moment when I made the stupidest remark I'd ever made up until that point. "There's The Swallow just a mile or so along this road, but it's a bit expensive."

McCartney didn't miss a beat. "Money no object," he said.

That afternoon we cleared all the tables and chairs, and somewhere around five hundred of us paid 50p each to cram into the dining room of Havelock Hall to hear Wings play. They performed a whole lot of old rock and roll favourites like "Lucille" and "Jonnie B Goode," and the night was brilliant and memorable. It also made a good front page headline story for The Courier.

These were the days when every news story had to be typed out in separate paragraphs on individual A5 sheets of paper, followed by a careful word count to ensure that the article could fit into the space provided on the designated page. We had a basic photo library and quite a few volunteers taking new pictures, and so sorting the head-lines and lay-out was all good fun. The highlight of my week was to heap everything we needed into a large bag, load it up in one of the students' union's two transit mini-buses, and set off west and across the River Tyne towards the printers who were based in Consett in County Durham. This was a whole further education.

Consett was, at that time, a steel-town, by which I mean that the primary, if not the sole reason for its existence was the steel mill. But this wasn't just an ordinary steel mill. I don't think I was ever told the reason, but there was something about the industrial process which produced a fine red dust which poured out of the vast mill chimneys, thereby polluting the air and settling on absolutely every living thing and inanimate object for miles around. You could quite literally see Consett over the horizon when approaching it. You'd be driving across rather wild but nonetheless beautiful moorland when suddenly, in the distance, you'd see what looked like a huge and dense column of bright red, stretching up into the clouds, which were therefore now a strange hue of grey and rust. Usually in the rain. When you came closer and in among the streets, it was impossible to ignore the fine red dust over buildings, windows, cars, clothes lines full of washing, dogs, cats and of course people. Only God knows what must have been the toll taken in bad health and consequent misery for generations ingesting the red dust from the Consett steelworks. Fortunately for me, I was in and out for a few hours once a week, but Christ Almighty.

I'd arrive with all the stories and photographs, have the rise taken out of me for several hours by the local printers on account of my by now foot-long hair and cissy embroidered T-shirts, and then head off home with maybe five hundred copies of the latest edition of the paper.

Running the university newspaper meant that inevitably I was involved in student politics, and it gradually emerged that I might be a candidate for the sabbatical role of President of the Students' Union and Students' Representative Council. Truth to tell, such had been the disproportionate time and energy spent on my journalistic life as opposed to my academic efforts, that I feared that success in the election might be the only way I'd be able to keep my place in the final year. The department would hardly be likely to throw out the President-elect, and if I got through the sabbatical year successfully, I'd be able to dedicate myself properly to studies for the final stages of my degree.

Luckily for me, that's what happened. There was one other candidate who seemed to be a bit of a Tory but whose constituency consisted mostly of the vast School of Agriculture. There was someone else from "Soc. soc." whose politics made Mao look like a squeamish moderate. And me, a long-haired lout from the soft left who stood a chance of attracting votes from anyone who didn't want to cast their ballot in favour of either of the other two. I won and there followed the best year of my short life to date, spent organising and leading demos against Ted Heath's government, chairing debates on everything from boycotting imports from South Africa to women's right to choose, negotiating with the university on behalf of the students, and enjoying getting to know quite a few girlfriends.

Having already given myself a well-deserved verbal birching for my filial ingratitude, I think it's fair to say that my mum and dad did enjoy some upside from my student years when they were invited to be among the VIP guests at the annual Presidents' Ball, which took place at Newcastle's rather grand Civic Centre. It took the shape of a formal dinner followed by entertainment and dancing, and was the only grand occasion of the year other than graduation. As the host and chair, I made a speech to the assembled crowd, and I think it might have been one of few occasions up until that point when the folks felt a bit of pride in their otherwise useless son. I hope so.

I'm a big believer that any successful career involves a lot of work, but also a lot of luck, and there's no doubt that winning the election and spending a year as President of the Union was the first of a number of very lucky breaks which came along in my lifetime. Had I not been successful, I've little doubt that I'd have been prevented from finishing my degree and would then have been thrown onto the jobs market with no useful skills or qualifications more marketable than my A level in Divinity. As it was I finished my degree, and being able to write "editor of the students' newspaper" and "President of the Students' Union" on my CV no doubt marked me out when future job and other opportunities appeared on my radar.

It also occurs to me that at this point the reader might be thinking that I'm being unduly self-deprecating in an attempt to ingratiate myself through humility. "You make your own luck," I hear some of you saying. So for the sake of historical accuracy, and in order to prove my underlying point that at this time I was an actual idiot, I should confess that during this period I got married. Yep. Maybe only 21 years old, without a brain cell in my head, I fell in love with a beautiful young woman, asked her to marry me, and got wed. There. I've said it.

I won't add to the many disservices I've done to this very nice and very able person by identifying her at this stage. She went on after our divorce to marry again, gave birth to two lovely boys, and to pursue a worthwhile and impressive career. I read recently that she'd even received a medal from the Queen. Well, she bloody well deserved one for the two years or so that she was involved with me. When I met and fell in love with a different young woman who'd been her contemporary at school, and left and divorced her, her mother might easily have killed me. As it was she prayed to her God for something terrible to happen to me and, despite the fact that she soon relented and withdrew her request, it was too late. Her prayers were going to be answered, but all that was still a little way in the future.

When the time approached for upcoming graduates to apply for a job, I went to the Careers Advice Bureau in the university to seek their counsel. I was met by a grey man with grey hair wearing grey whom we'll call Mr Grey. "What do you want to do?" he asked. "I thought I might try journalism," I replied. Mr Grey shook his head and sucked his teeth. "You too?" he said, and nodded in the general direction of a large filing cabinet fashioned from attractive grey metal. "That's all the information we've got about jobs in journalism. Good luck."

My ambition at this stage was sufficiently vague and unfocused that I didn't even have a clear idea of whether I wanted to aim for newspaper or broadcast journalism. Leafing through the well-thumbed A4 sheets, I came across an application for an apprenticeship scheme run by Thomson newspapers, and also what seemed to be an ancient leaflet describing a Graduate Training Scheme run by the BBC. I extracted the pages and took them back to Mr Grey, who glanced at them and snickered.

'You'll be lucky," he said. "The BBC has been running the scheme for about ten years. They only take a handful of people a year and so far as I know they've only ever taken people from Oxford or Cambridge." Never being one to let very poor odds or an asshole rain on my parade, I nevertheless asked for a photocopy of the application form and set off to the library to fill it in.

I'm grateful to an enterprising executive from the then fast-growing computer company called Burroughs Machines who had seen me participating in a debate shown on Tyne Tees Television, and approached me with the offer of a job. Among the attractions was that their star salesman had bought himself a new Toyota sports car with the commission he'd earned in just one month. Among the less attractive aspects was that in your first week you'd be given a basic desk-top adding machine which in those days was about the same size and weight as a golf-ball typewriter (what's that? – ed), and told to go door to door on an industrial estate until you managed to find someone stupid enough to buy it. Such was my naivety and lack of self-knowledge that I was even considering this possibility, when to my amazement I received a letter inviting me to an interview at the BBC. Good heavens, I thought, I'd better listen to some of their news programmes.

I schlepped down to London on the evening before the appointed day and stayed overnight with my parents in Beckenham. Quite what they made of the possibility that their son might get a job working for the BBC will never be known, but they seemed to be taking it in their stride. By this time I was sporting a slightly more sensible hair-cut and my year as student president had required the acquisition of a reasonable suit, so maybe I looked more like a serious candidate than I felt. In the morning I successfully managed to navigate the under-ground and, as I emerged into the dingy daylight on the corner of Oxford Circus, I felt a strong surge of what I now know to be called imposter syndrome. I'd managed to bluff my way through quite a lot by the age of twenty-two, but what on earth did I think I was playing at imagining I could get a job at the BBC? With these undermining thoughts rattling around my head, I found my way to Broadcasting House in Portland Place, where I was met by a very nice man and a very nice woman who were polite and encouraging, and explained that they were doing preliminary interviews with a view to compiling a short-list of candidates to be seen by the full panel. I have no recall of the content of the discussion, but I think I must have emerged feeling that I'd acquitted myself reasonably well. More importantly,

I'd been left in little doubt that it might be a good idea to listen to or watch one or two of the BBC's news programmes in case I should be invited for a second interview.

I'm not sure that I was quite as amazed as I should have been that I was invited back. I learned later that some four thousand people had applied for the available places, and I don't think I realised quite how fortunate I had been to get to this last hurdle. In fact I'm sure I can't have, because otherwise I would no doubt have embarked on a more systematic project of listening to the Today programme, The World at One, PM, and the various bulletins on TV.

Well what can I tell you, other than that the second interview was an ordeal. You know those nightmares about facing an important exam tomorrow and not having done the revision? That's what it was like, but in real life. There were no fewer than eight people on the other side of the table, representing TV news, network radio news, the World Service, the foreign desks, local radio, Ceefax, etc etc. Each of them asked their questions in turn, rather in the manner of a US Senate hearing in which sarcastic politicians pretend to be even more sarcastic prosecuting barristers. No, apparently I hadn't listened to the World Service; indeed I'd be hard pressed to know how to find it on the dial. No, I had never been a regular listener to BBC Radio Newcastle when I was there at university, and no, I hadn't gone along to said local radio station to offer my services as a volunteer. In fact so lacking in initiative and enterprise was I that the thought of volunteering had never even occurred to me. The best I could do was to offer some thoughts on the one-minute bulletin of world news run on Radio One on the half hour, and the similar two-minute bulletin on Radio Two. When they'd established that I didn't have any meaningful questions to ask them, I positively fled from the room and, once outside, found myself leaning back on the wall to regain my breath and composure. I was in a cold sweat and my heart was beating like something that beats fast and noisily. The very nice secretary sitting quietly behind her desk looked concerned and gave me an encouraging smile.

"I wouldn't worry too much," she said, "you're the first person who's come out of there today who isn't crying."

In view of all that, you'll be as astonished as I was that I got a place on the scheme. I learned later that someone inside the BBC had pointed out that they'd seldom if ever taken a graduate from anywhere other than Oxbridge, and that maybe it was time to widen their catchment. Someone from a redbrick university with pronounced south London vowels, but who'd at least edited the student newspaper and served as president of the union, might fit the bill. See what I mean about luck?

AND SO IT BEGINS

The BBC's journalists' training scheme was a very privileged programme, in which we fortunate few were given a series of three-month
attachments to various parts of the Corporation. The idea was that
you'd learn whatever each place had to teach you, and at an appropriate moment you'd apply for a full time role in one of them. We all
started off based at Broadcasting House where we were given formal
lessons in law as it applies to journalism, in how local government
works, and once per week we were shunted across the road to the
Langham (before it was an hotel) where a wonderful woman called
Florence Carter attempted to teach us a simplified form of shorthand
called T-line. Visits were arranged to local councils and crown courts
and coroner's courts, where the officiating coroner memorably closed
the session at the end of the day and talked us through a series of his
more macabre cases. One in particular involved a lot of rope and silk
scarves; another involved a skeleton abandoned in an attic and a swarm
of fat cockroaches. You know the kind of thing.

These were the days before regional accents were as welcomed
and celebrated as they are today, and we were subjected to a session
with a BBC radio newsreader who doubled as the person whose job it
was to humiliate anyone who had sneaked in from the lower classes.
Each of us in turn was required to read out a prescribed section of a

bulletin while Mr Sneer listened carefully. "How," he asked me, "do you pronounce the word that is spelled T O T T E N H A M?" I could see the problem coming but seemed powerless to do anything about it. "Erm, Tot-en-ham?" I ventured three separate syllables. Mr Sneer sneered, and made it clear that if I harboured any hope to become a newsreader or reporter on the BBC, I'd be obliged to find a way to lose my south London vowels. I remember my friend Joan Bakewell saying that after she felt herself to be an outsider at Cambridge, she went into the ladies' room speaking with a working-class Stockport accent and came out with an upper-class southern one. I think I did something similar (though not, of course, in any way involving the ladies' room.)

My first attachment after the formal training was to what they called the Spur in White City to work on what was then the news on BBC2. I was very fortunate to be assigned to a shift managed by one of the few duty editors who did not resent new graduates on the grounds that we were being fast-tracked and feather-bedded through a system they'd had to navigate the hard way. He was an Australian (or maybe a New Zealander?) and I think his name was Dick Ross. On my first day there he kindly gave me a proper job looking after a suitably minor story which seemed likely to make the closing stages of the late bulletin. Stories were typed with one paragraph per page, with the "story-slug" in one corner, and the name of the sub-editor looking after it in the other. I can't now remember the actual subject, but I do remember watching my copy being passed to the news editor who read it carefully, nodded, and then handed it to the newsreader who was none other than the magnificent Angela Rippon. I can still feel the frisson of excitement I experienced when I encountered Angela Rippon for the first time. She was among the first famous people I'd ever come across, and was certainly the most glamourous. I watched as my story reached the top of her pile to look through, she picked it up, scanned the words and the slug, and then her eyes alighted on my name.

"Who's Stuart Prebble?" I heard her say, but in more or less the tone you'd use if enquiring about an obnoxious smell. "That's me," I stuttered, "is everything okay?" I don't think she actually answered, and I was happy to take her silence as reassurance that I hadn't messed up. I'd had my stories read aloud on the radio before this, but this was the first time one of them had been read with the authoritative and unmistakeable delivery of Angela Rippon. I couldn't wait to tell my mum.

On the same shift on BBC1, and so on duty when I was, was my friend Robin. But Robin, unfortunately for him, was working for an editor who held graduate trainees in contempt. We'll call him Jack Schyte. Jack seemed determined not to give Robin anything useful to do, until one day a more senior editor intervened and instructed Schyte to allocate him a task. With bad grace, he gave Robin the job of preparing a caption and filling in the blanks indicating the result of an important football match which was due to finish just before the end of that evening's bulletin. He'd have to take a call from a stringer at the ground, tell the graphics people the score, and write it on the script and autocue. That's all he had to do.

You can probably guess what happened. If you have twenty things to do in a day, you'll get them all right. If you have one thing to do … so of course on the actual bulletin, the caption said Chelsea 2, Liverpool 3, and the newsreader read Chelsea 3, Liverpool 2. Oh. My. God.

Jack Schyte emerged from the control room, flung down his scripts, and let the entire newsroom know that his previous opinion of good-for-nothing trainees had been acquitted. If the ground could have opened up and swallowed Robin, he would have dived into the chasm. If the windows had opened wide enough, he would have been found sprawled in a mulch of blood and gore on the carpark below. As it was he was simply mortified, lost for an explanation, and more wretched than he'd ever felt in his entire life. Poor sod, who went on the have a long and highly distinguished career in journalism. As for Jack Schyte? He continued forever to be a nobody.

Undeterred by events on the other shift, my editor Dick Ross continued to give me opportunities, and after a few days he allocated me the task of overseeing the editing of a filmed report for the lunchtime news bulletin. The piece had just come in from Simon Dring, who was reporting from the front line of the conflict going on in Cyprus between Greeks and Turks. I was directed towards an area filled with Acmade cutting machines, and I introduced myself to the editor. You couldn't exactly call it an exchange of pleasantries, and I took a seat alongside the editing machine and waited for what would happen next. Notebook in hand I waited a minute, then another minute, and still the editor was sitting back and doing nothing.

"Is there something wrong?" I asked. "Something I need to do?"

The editor said nothing, but simply pointed to the corner of the Acmade, where my right hand was resting on the edge of the machine. Still momentarily confused, I then realised that he wasn't going to start work while I was actually touching it. I removed my hand and he got going. "Unions rules," he said, and that was as close as I got to an explanation.

The first shots on the 16mm film were taken from behind three soldiers inside a barricade. One of them got to his feet, fired off three live rounds from his rifle, and then ducked down out of harm's way. Up popped Simon who started talking to the camera. He said words along the lines of, "Here on the front line of the increasingly bitter dispute between two sides who used to be neighbours ..." but then he fluffed a word and said (something like) "damn". Take two, and our cameraman is still inside the barricade behind three soldiers, one of them stands up and fires three shots into the distance, and then Simon comes into frame and starts his piece to camera. Which is not to say that Simon was making anything up, and indeed this same reporter was later injured while still reporting from Cyprus, but I learned at least two important lessons on that day. One, not everything you see on television is what it seems, and two, the broadcasting trade unions were living on borrowed time.

Very early on a Monday morning a few weeks later I was on my way in my VW Beetle up the motorway to report for duty at Radio Stoke on Trent, and at 1pm on that same day, I was sitting in their studio presenting the main half-hour long news programme. Was this because I was the best and most qualified person available to present this flagship programme? No, it was because I was the *only* person available to present the programme.

The relevant head of news was an excellent bloke called Tony Inchley, and is one of a number of terrific people to whom I owe a great deal, because he gave me every possible chance to learn and to prove myself, and taught me some very important lessons in journalism.

I was staying for bed and breakfast in Mrs Rose's guest house where I was sharing a room with a plumber who had recently left his wife and seemed to be making up for lost time by dating and sleeping with every woman between the ages of forty-five and ninety within a five mile radius of Hanley. I didn't ever actually meet him for the first two weeks we were sharing a room, because he'd arrive home after I'd gone to sleep, and I was always out on the early shift before he woke up. I think we eventually met one Sunday and he took me out to what turned into the most ghastly social evening I'd ever spent in my life up to that point. It all happened at some sort of club where there seemed to be an unspoken agreement that all the local married women were there to have sex with someone other than their husbands, and all the local married men were there to oblige. One of those evenings you spend quite a lot of time trying to obliterate from your memory, which I more or less have. I only remember that it was messy.

BBC Radio Stoke had an early shift and a late shift, and it suited me because I had little or nothing else to do, to work both. After the morning news programmes, a radio DJ would take to the airwaves with chat and requests and light music, and at some time around mid-morning he would trail the upcoming news programme, cutting live to the newsroom where Tony Inchley would be ready to outline the stories we were all working on for the full news programme at lunchtime.

The main news on one particular day was the appalling weather conditions on the M6 motorway, where the police had reported a series of accidents caused, it was said, by motorists travelling too fast in poor visibility. As Tony was speaking, in walked one of our reporters called Tim, who lived in Birmingham and had therefore (thought Tony) just driven up that very stretch of road. Without missing a beat, he introduced the prospect of an "arriving now from the scene" live report, and may have just about had time to wonder why Tim was waving his hands as though mimicking uncoordinated windscreen wipers and mouthing "no", but it was too late. Tony handed the microphone to Tim, who also didn't miss a beat. "Yes Tony, there've been scores of pile ups, and emergency services have been pleading with lorry drivers in particular to check their speed. The weather fore-casters are predicting that conditions will improve later on, but for the moment the message is, slow down and take extra care." He returned the mic to Tony who glanced out of the window and looked upwards at the sky. "And the weather?" he said, "dry with sunny periods, and the chance of the odd shower later on." Then he tidily ended up the trailer and turned back to Tim to ask what was the problem? "I had a skinful in the local pub last night," said Tim, "and ended up sleeping under the desk in the studio."

Later I asked Tony about the provenance of the apparently spon-taneous weather forecast. "I just looked at the sky," said Tony, "'dry with sunny periods, a chance of an odd shower later on,' fits the bill about ninety per cent of the time."

One evening a few weeks later I was on the late shift, during which my job was to prepare enough stories to populate the bulletin which would be broadcast early the following morning. This usually involved making increasingly desperate calls to the police, ambulance and fire services, seeking information about any incident, no matter how trivial, that might make a story. Relations between the local radio and local emergency services are usually cordial, but I'd always find myself irritated when they'd answer my enquiry with the words "nothing newsworthy". "You put out the fires, I'll decide what's newsworthy." Of course I mouthed it silently but never actually said it aloud.

This particular evening was as dead as the grave and even at my most inventive I could think of little or nothing to leave for the early-morning man to read in his bulletins. Finally in desperation, Tim and I decided to go to the pub, have a few drinks, and then come back to make some late calls in the hope that by then something newsworthy would have happened. So that's what we did, except that we didn't have a few drinks, we had a lot of drinks, and it was near midnight by the time I stumbled back into the newsroom and began making my calls. The first was to the fire brigade. "Anything newsworthy?" I asked. "I was going to try to call you," came the answer, "there's a massive fire going on right now down at the (something or other) mill. It's out of control and they're evacuating the area."

Suddenly alert and quickly sobering up, I put down the receiver, grabbed my tape recorder and hurried to my Beetle. Of course I was well over the legal limit, but that didn't seem as important as getting to the incident. From some distance away I could see the sky lit up by the flames, giving off huge billowing clouds of smoke. When I got still closer, it looked like one of those scenes from wartime footage of the Blitz, in which intrepid fire-fighters lean back in groups to support each other to counter the force of their jets of water. I drove in between the fire engines and firemen as far as I could, turned off the engine, started my tape-recorder, got out of the car and started walking. All while as drunk as a skunk.

"And as I'm approaching the blaze," I said, "all around me I can see brave fire-fighters struggling to aim huge jets of water into the seat of the flames. The air is full of acrid smoke, and the sky is illuminated for what seems like miles around with a red, orange and yellow hue, and just along the road I can see teams of police escorting local residents, many of them still wearing their dressing gowns, to safety." I then started interviewing the chief fire officer who was directing the operation.

Eventually at about 3am I took my tapes back to the newsroom, did a quick edit, sent it to London and went back to Mrs Rose's guest house to sleep the sleep of the Righteous. When I arrived back in the newsroom later that morning, I was greeted by a round of applause from colleagues. My drunken adventure, which occurred only because I'd gone to the pub instead of persevering to finish the bulletin, had led the national morning news and I was a one-day hero.

My next attachment took me to regional television in Leeds where I worked in the newsroom alongside the then presenter Michael Cooke, and the very able TV reporter Jeremy Thompson (latterly of Sky News). Once again I was given every opportunity to prove myself, and was soon to be found fronting on-camera reports for the local evening news on Look North. Early one afternoon we received word of a serious coach crash at a place called Dibbles Bridge in North Yorkshire. The only available proper reporter, Ken Cooper, was sent to the scene, and I was sent to the hospital where the injured were due to be ferried. The exact timings have gone out of my head, but I know that we were under terrible pressure to get something back for the evening news, which meant hurrying to the location, shooting whatever we could see within a few minutes, piling back in the car, speeding back to Leeds, getting the film into processing, doing a quick edit, and getting it on the air. With all the pressure and adrenalin, it's difficult to focus on the reality for the families of victims of Britain's worst ever road accident. Thirty-three people killed at the scene, and it was my first appearance on the national television news. What can you say?

My first full time job took me back to my university city of Newcastle, where I was appointed as a regional journalist working on the local version of Look North, presented by the magnificent Mike Neville and covering the whole area of the north-east and Cumbria.

Once again I embarked on a work schedule which sometimes involved getting up at 5am to go into the newsroom to write and then read the morning bulletins, then heading home for a quick shower and bite to eat, then back in for the 10am daily news conference, going out again to film, script and edit one, two or even three separate news reports for Look North, and then quite often staying on to do a final report for the (then) 9 o'clock news or Newsnight. Then the same again tomorrow. Was I exhausted? Yes. Was it great fun? Yes again.

I think I was probably an energetic and reasonably presentable reporter, but my fame and popularity was suddenly out of all proportion to my talent simply because I regularly sat next to Mike Neville, who was the legendary and much-loved anchor-man of the show. For a long time Mike was in the Guinness Book of Records as the longest-standing TV news presenter in the world, and it's fair to say that his friendly, funny and endearing style made him a household name throughout the region. Everywhere I'd go, people would ask "how's Mike?" and tell me an anecdote about how they'd seen him in a pub or shopping in his local supermarket. He and a co-anchor George House used to present a very funny stage-show called "Larn yersel' Geordie," which packed in the crowds. Mike would come in to work at about 4pm each day, look through the stories, present the show at 6pm, and then at 6.30 he'd go to the BBC Club and work his way slowly through a bottle of Scotch. Every night. Then he'd drive home.

So famous and so beloved was Mike that the local police knew his habits and would sometimes discreetly escort his car through the streets to his home in Whickham. All of which was fine until one day a traffic officer who was new to the region and didn't know its ways, stopped Mike and breathalysed him. Mike was banned from driving for a year, and none of the poor young officer's colleagues ever spoke to him again.

One day in 1975 I was asked by the national news team in London to cover a speech that the Prime Minister Harold Wilson was due to make at Newcastle City Hall. Wilson had been PM for six years up until 1970, then had lost to Ted Heath, but was now in the second year of his second term. In those days a politician would hand out advance copies of their speeches to reporters, so that we could be sure not to have run out of film by the time they got to the most newsworthy parts. However when I asked Mr Wilson for a copy of his speech, he said he didn't have one.

"So how will I know which bit to record for the news?" I asked him.

"You'll know," he said and calmly took the stage.

We duly positioned ourselves at the back of the hall and waited as Harold Wilson addressed an audience of perhaps a thousand people. He spoke in unremarkable and measured tones for maybe ten minutes, and then apropos of nothing else, in the middle of his speech he said, "turn over." Turn over is what reporters and directors say to camera-operators when they want to start filming, so we did, and at that moment Wilson made a gear-change of volume and animation, and proceeded to damn the iniquitous former Tory government with all his force and might. The colourful invective lasted for about forty-five seconds, at which point his tirade returned to normal just as suddenly as it had started. I had my news-clip, and the media had been successfully manipulated. Quite what the wider audience in the hall had made of the words "turn over" in the middle of Wilson's speech, one can only guess at.

There was widespread amazement when, just a year later, it was announced one afternoon that Wilson was standing down as Prime

Minister. Everyone was taken by surprise and the London newsroom was urgently seeking reaction from all the main players in politics and the trade unions. Word reached us that the highly influential leader of the National Union of Mineworkers, Joe Gormley, was at that moment on a plane which was due to land in Newcastle in half an hour. I was dispatched with a film crew to meet him, and we ran the cameras as I approached him on the tarmac and told him "Harold Wilson's resigned." "Good God," he said, and it was clear that, like everyone else, he'd had no idea. Wilson's action gave rise to widespread speculation about his reasons, including that he was secretly a KGB agent, that he was the victim of an MI5 plot, or that he had been given a diagnosis of Alzheimer's. To this day there seems to be no certain answer.

Then two years later, in 1978, when James Callaghan was Prime Minister, I had my first meeting with Margaret Thatcher, who by then was Leader of the Opposition. She was visiting the nuclear reprocessing plant at Windscale in West Cumbria, which was a constant source of controversy because of the regular reports of minor leaks, and also of local anxiety about the potentially catastrophic consequences of a major accident. My main memory is of her bustling around at twice the walking speed of anyone trying to keep up with her, proselytising about the wonders of nuclear energy, and impatiently dismissing any of my questions which might hint at doubt or misgivings.

It wasn't all quite so serious. It was in this period that President Jimmy Carter initiated what he called the Friendship Force, in which Newcastle found itself twinned with Atlanta Georgia, an event marked by a glorious ceremonial visit by the President himself. Of course the Secret Service kept us at a distance, but I did manage a shouted question and got an indecipherable answer for my trouble. The region enjoyed a visit from a still more exalted guest when the legendary Ella Fitzgerald came to perform at the Newport Jazz Festival at Ayresome Park football ground in Middlesbrough. On that occasion I fared better, managing to grab a brief interview as she waited in the wings before taking the stage. I have a sneaking suspicion that she was irritated by my timing, but she indulged my stupidity and managed to remain both polite and regal.

As well as the regional news, presented in BBC programmes such as Look North, Points West, Look East, each of the (then) fifteen ITV regions used to produce a range of other programmes reflecting the local community back to itself. It's difficult to grasp the importance of this if you live in London, but if you don't, seeing all your news from the perspective of the capital city can be irritating. Someone boiling a double-yolk egg for breakfast in Camden can be deemed more important than a biblical flood where you live, and providing some regional balance used to be part of the raison d'etre of the ITV system. Even in BBC North-East, in addition to the evening news, we used to produce two half-hour features a week in which we would opt out of the network service to cover something of more local interest. It was this service which gave me my first ever opportunity to get involved in some half-hour programmes when one of the producers called David Seymour brought me in to present two shows he was making. David had been a famous and successful presenter himself, but was now working behind the scenes producing local opt-outs.

David had decided to look again at a notorious gangland crime which had taken place in the region in 1967 and was known, memorably, as "The One-Armed Bandit Murder." Two men, Dennis Stafford and Michael Luvaglio had been convicted of killing a local gangster called Angus Sibbet and were given life sentences. Michael was the younger brother of another well-known local gangster called Vince Landa who ran slot machines in the north-east, and the killing is believed to have inspired the film Get Carter featuring Michael Caine. Both Michael Luvaglio and Dennis Stafford had loudly protested their innocence throughout, and while possibly neither of them was a model citizen, there was reason to think the men might not have committed this particular crime.

It was a one of those classic and perfect-for-telly stories which involved reconstructing the crime by driving flashy cars through dark streets, and casting doubt on whether the two accused could have been where the police said they were in order to have committed the murder. It was all going well and I was enjoying the whole process, when one day it occurred to me that while one of the convicted men, Michael Luvaglio, probably hadn't committed the murder, the other one, Dennis Stafford, almost certainly had. What was more, when you looked closely at the evidence, it was pretty obvious.

Immediately troubled, I went to see David Seymour and said something like, "we're about to produce a programme claiming that these two men are innocent, and we know that one of them probably isn't." His response was something along the lines of, "Just be grateful that I'm involving you in my programmes and try not to be a naïve idiot."

So now I'm in a tricky situation. This is my first opportunity to present two half-hour programmes. Sometimes these shows made in the BBC regions get a network airing, so it's a big deal for me. On the other hand we're in the process of presenting a story which I don't actually believe to be true. I've already upset the producer by raising the matter with him and am at risk of irritating him still further if I pursue it. After agonising for a few days, I decide to seek advice from the head of regional features in the north-east, John Mapplebeck. I ask to see John privately and tell him of my concerns. "Please don't tell David I've raised this with you," I said, "because I've already made him angry, but I'm just not sure what's the best thing to do." John said something like "leave it with me," and the next thing I knew was that I was summoned across the road to see David Seymour who went ballistic. He'd taken a chance bringing me into this project and how could I be so ungrateful? Who did I think I was? How did I dare to go behind his back? Basically my career in TV journalism was over before it had started.

All this seems like a storm in a very small teacup right now, but it's amazing the extent to which it can spoil your day at the time. I'm certain that if most of the programmes had not been filmed already, I would have been edited out of them. As it was, David completed the programmes with all the appropriate checks and balances which undoubtedly would have been the case without the benefit of my intervention; they aired on two consecutive Tuesdays and made not the slightest difference to anyone or anything. I've absolutely no doubt that David had acted with total editorial integrity throughout, and he went on to be appointed as the BBC's regional television manager in the north-east.

Notwithstanding this unfortunate debacle, my career as an on-screen reporter for BBC North East was going well. I was increasingly famous, and was even occasionally asked to host an entertainment event or open a fete. I compered a variety spectacular in Blyth featuring the comedian Dickie Henderson, and drove like a maniac after the show one day to crown the Berwick Salmon Queen. My second wife Marilyn was working as a secretary in BBC publications and was pursuing a career as a model. She was featured in photospreads in several local newspapers and magazines and was well on her way to what promised to become a highly successful career. Our joy was unconfined when she became pregnant with our first child, and we looked forward to parenthood with all the enthusiasm of any couple who feel very blessed and have no reason to spend much time wondering what could go wrong.

BIRTHS AND DEATHS

Alex was a big bump, probably made even bigger because Marilyn was naturally slender, but took the advice she was given to drink a bottle of Guinness now and then because it was good for the baby. Her pregnancy was normal and happy, and we used to joke that her developing shape was like a knot in a piece of string. The baby was late by two weeks in announcing her arrival, and what was intended by Marilyn to be a natural birth gradually and then urgently turned into an impossibly extended and painful labour eventually lasting thirty hours, and finally involving an epidural and forceps. The whole thing was a trauma for all concerned, and of course it's impossible to imagine or even properly to empathise with what it must have been like for Marilyn. But eventually the miracle took place, our daughter emerged, there was a loud wail, and we all joined in with a deep sigh of relief. Marilyn had been to hell and back and instantly fell into a deep sleep. It was 4am on 5th October 1979 and I felt as though I'd been hit by a truck, but I was a dad.

I went to sleep for two hours, and then went to work, did a full day, and got a celebratory name-check on the show that evening (because of course I'd done all the hard work). When I returned to the hospital, Marilyn was wide awake and nursing our baby daughter. Alex was slow to crawl but quick to walk, slow with small motor movements but quick to learn to read, and began to grow up with the sunny and happy disposition which she still exhibits today, and is one of the several reasons why a lot of people love her.

The three hundred miles distance between my parents' home in Beckenham and ours in Newcastle meant that family visits were rare but Mum absolutely loved having a granddaughter. She had suffered for many years with various ailments which at that time were described to me euphemistically as "women's issues," and which she most definitely did not want to talk about. Despite her increasing discomfort and then pain, she adamantly resisted seeking medical intervention. I've little doubt that this was partly due to the widespread reluctance among that generation for "troubling the doctor," it was partly because of her general fear of hospitals, but mostly it was because Mum was terrified to hear the C word, assuming at that it meant a slow, painful and inevitable death, which in those days it usually did.

When the situation became beyond negotiation and Mum was eventually examined, the doctors at first informed my dad that his wife was suffering from stomach cancer. This was right at the top of their list of worst fears, and he was certain that if Mum learned of the diagnosis, she would instantly go into a further decline, sapping her morale and will to fight. He insisted that while the prescribed treatment should go ahead, she should not be allowed to hear the specific word. Amazingly this worked for a while, and Mum endured and tolerated the prescribed cancer treatment for several months until the day when a doctor on a routine ward-round spelled out her diagnosis. Whether he did so accidentally or deliberately is unknown, and he probably has no idea how close he came to being punched by my dad. Whatever the motive or intent, what's undeniable is that from that moment onward Mum's spirit and will went into the steepest dive imaginable. She was terrified beyond all reasoning, she completely lost hope, and her most earnest and desperate wish was to be allowed to take to her bed at home and die there without any further medical interference.

Shortly after the revelation, I received a call from my dad telling me what had happened, and asking me if I could come down urgently to see her. Apparently she was desperate to speak to me in person. I caught the train and sat at her bedside as she told me that she had begged my dad to help her to end her life, but that he had declared that he was unable to do so. She was imploring me to try to persuade him, and if that proved impossible, please could I help her myself. I find myself incapable of writing any words which would come close to accurately describing what I was feeling as I listened to what she had to say. You could close your eyes and try to put yourself in a similar situation, but I don't recommend it.

Downstairs, and while Mum was sleeping, I discussed the matter with my dad, and was not surprised that he would not and could not countenance her request. Leaving aside that he would be likely to go to jail, and then leaving aside the fact that he would have no idea how to go about the task, he simply could not bring himself to end the life of the woman he'd been married to for thirty odd years. I understood, and made no effort to persuade him.

If all this had happened ten or fifteen years later, when I was a bit older and wiser, and maybe assisted suicide was more discussed, I like to think I would have acquiesced in the last thing she would ever ask me. As it was, I was thirty and did not have the first idea how one would go about such a thing even if I could bring myself to do it. I'm sorry to have to say that, not for the first time, I let Mum down.

When eventually Dad and the nursing team could no longer manage her pain and medical needs at home, the idea was mooted that Mum should go into a hospice. This was, of course, St Christopher's, and was the hospice in which I had worked, and the sole purpose of which was therefore impossible to disguise. Mum could not have been more horrified if someone had told her that she was being dispatched into hell itself, but at that moment and in those circumstances there simply was no choice. Dad was at the end of his resilience, and even administering the essential pain-management was outside his current competence. After the dreadful trauma of her transfer, Mum was quickly out of pain for the first time in months, and when I went to see her in the clean, bright, cheerful environment I remembered, it was clear that this was where she needed to be. I think that perhaps it was a week or so later that Dad and I were told that she was in no imminent danger, but were then awoken by that phone call in the small hours of the morning. On this occasion they were not calling to tell us to hurry in; they were calling to tell us that Mum had passed, peacefully, in her sleep, aged just fifty-four. Dad was in the kitchen at that moment, where he picked up a cloth and started wiping down the already pristine draining board. "Oh well, he said, "better get on," and then he dropped the cloth and fell into my arms, sobbing. Unless I am mistaken, I think it was the first time he and I had ever hugged.

When facing death, as in the rest of her life, Mum's first consideration had been for me rather than for herself. She had written a letter telling me what a wonderful son I had been. I hadn't.

My mum deserves about ninety per cent of the credit for anything worthwhile I've ever achieved in my life. Whatever my upbringing may have lacked in material terms was made up for one hundred-fold by being the focus of her totally unselfish and unconditional love. I don't doubt that this is what provided the foundation of any self-confidence I may have acquired, and I'll be sure to let her know that properly when I see her in the next life.

MEANWHILE ...

—

I was doing quite a lot of work for the national news at this point, mostly covering stories of industrial action among miners or in the shipyards. I went to London for a few short attachments working for the 9 O'Clock News, where I was regularly assigned to the least important stories of any day, and was always the one required to stay late until after all bulletins had gone out "just in case". A rare exception was in November 1978 when I was sent to report on the last edition of The Times before a long running dispute involving printers and journalists was causing the newspaper group to close down. Scouring the local pubs where journalists were drowning their sorrows, I was surprised to come across the actor Jack Nicholson, considerably the worse for wear. With the camera running, I asked him how he came to be here. He looked back at me under half-closed eyelids and drawled, "I just love to come to funerals."

Late one evening I found myself sitting in the reporters' room with a veteran BBC correspondent called Larry Harris. Larry was nudging towards the end of what I'm sure had been a long and distinguished career in TV news, but now he wasn't feeling it. "I've been around the world three times," he said it in the same tone you might use if you'd been sentenced to Robben Island, "and I'm probably going around the world another three times." It was eleven o'clock at night, he was deep in his cups, and suddenly I had a premonition of what my life could easily be if I remained on the same path.

At any one time there are probably no more than about ten on-screen TV news reporters in the UK who are so revered and respected that they can more or less choose their own assignments, and I had enough self-knowledge to realise that I was unlikely ever to be one of them. At that moment I decided that I'd rather be the bloke behind the camera telling Larry Harris that we were sending him off to The Central African Republic, than the bloke being sent there by some snotty-nosed kid.

In those days it was very hard to move within the BBC from news to current affairs; it seemed to me that the elite producers based in Lime Grove would rather hire their nephews or nieces than anyone from the BBC News Graduate Training Scheme, and so I looked around for an alternative route leading in the direction I wanted to go. I'd always had a hankering to work on World in Action, but I knew they'd never hire me directly onto the team, so I made it my business to look for vacancies at Granada TV in Manchester where the show was based.

I applied for and got an interview for the job of news editor on the evening regional magazine programme Granada Reports, and when I got there they asked me the very obvious question; why does a potentially high-flying BBC news reporter want to work in a backroom job as a local news editor? I instantly 'fessed up that I didn't want the job, but that I wanted to work at Granada because I was keen to work on World in Action and was prepared to take a step backwards to get myself on the right ladder.

THE GRANADA YEARS

—

They took the point and offered me a job as an on-screen reporter on the evening news, on the understanding that I would be biding my time until I could move up to producing. When I asked what role they saw me playing in the reporting team, the Head of Regional Programmes Rod Caird said, "we want to achieve a situation in which, when you come up on the screen, viewers know that something important is going to happen." Good line huh? I was sold.

When I told the bosses at BBC North East that I was off to do a similar job at Granada, they thought I'd lost my mind. The Regional Television Manager Jim Graham no doubt meant well when he tried to dissuade me from going by telling me that I was just good enough to get away with it at BBC Newcastle, but that in Granada they'd chew me up and spit me out. His words redoubled my determination to go, and I did.

I felt a bit like a fish out of water on my first day at the morning news conference. Obviously everyone in the Manchester and Liverpool newsrooms was a hard-bitten and seasoned journalist, and I was fresh into the region and knew next to nothing about anything. A whole series of hard news stories were suggested and allocated to reporters, who sorted themselves out and set off like warriors going into the fray. At the end of the meeting the producers were looking for a light item to end the programme.

"There's the annual dog-show in Blackpool," said someone helpfully.

"Perfect," said the day-producer Andrew McLaughlin. "That'll be a good one for you Stuart."

Now I was in a dilemma. I'd been hired specifically on the basis that "when you come up on the screen, we want viewers to know that something important is going to happen," and here I was, on my first day, being asked to shoot a feature story about the Blackpool Dog Show. If I acquiesced, how would I ever be taken seriously? I waited for a few moments until McLaughlin returned to his office and went in to see him.

"About this Blackpool Dog Show," I said. "I'm afraid that's not what I was hired to do, so if you need it done, I'm sorry but you'll have to find someone else." Or words to that effect.

"Equally sorry," he said, "but that's the only story we need to have covered, and you're the only reporter we've got to cover it, so you need to go." Or words to that effect.

"Well that's very difficult then," I said, "because I'm not going."

I returned to my desk and was aware of a hurried conference on the other side of the glass window between newsroom and office, involving Andrew McLaughlin and Rod Caird, who'd hired me in the first place. Just about now I was contemplating the consequences of walking out of my new job on the very first day, thereby instantly giving validity to the dire warning I'd been given by the boss back in Newcastle, where I'd received a very nice on-screen farewell only three days earlier. And of course it wasn't completely irrelevant that I had a new family and bills to pay. After a tense quarter of an hour I was called in to see Rod, who asked me to sit down.

"I need to invite you to share a problem with me," he said. "I've got a new producer who's trying to assert his authority over his team and doesn't want me to undermine him, and I've got a very talented new reporter who is being asked to do a job he wasn't hired for. If you could find a way to help me out on this occasion, I'd be sure to remember it and be forever in your debt."

It was a very good speech, and one I've used with slight variations many times since. Of course I could only acquiesce, and I went to Blackpool and made what everyone later agreed was an entertaining report about how I had no idea why I'd been sent here because I hated dogs, and then walked away from camera pretending to wipe dog-shit off my shoe. That was my first day at Granada. I proceeded over the next few months to become a "nearly famous" but probably rather inconsequential face among the many beloved personalities on the screens of the north-west. I don't think anyone ever saw me pop up on the telly and thought, "something important is about to happen," but there we are. Andrew McLaughlin became one of my best mates and still is to this day.

Among the regular presenters of the regional news at the time was Bob Greaves, whose ubiquity on Granada screens had made him a local celebrity. He usually alternated with John Huntley who was and is a lovely and very talented broadcaster, and the brilliant Lucy Meacock who is still presenting the show thirty-five years later. Then they were both joined by Judy Finnigan who was young and talented and glamorous, and had a better and more direct connection with the viewing audience than any presenter I've ever worked with. A little later a new reporter joined the team from neighbouring Yorkshire TV – his name was Richard Madeley, and the rest you know. Richard and Judy went on to marry and become the most successful husband and wife presenting team in UK broadcasting history. Both amazingly talented, kind and generous people, and I love them.

Richard and Judy were not the only people for whom the particular environment of working in telly encouraged a close attachment. Every day in the news business involves a gradual build-up of excitement and pressure which reaches its peak at the time of transmission, and the urge to wind down with a drink after the show can be difficult to resist. Most of us were young, and our jobs involved long hours and lots of time spent away from home; consequently there was lots of opportunity. Maybe it's just an excuse, but it also felt that being part of the same creative team which regularly produced highs and lows, in many cases created a particular bond. Certainly there were many examples in our industry of professional relationships blurring with personal relationships, and a great many marriages suffered as a result. Mine included.

One of the important stories we were covering at the time was about the series of dreadful murders being carried out across the north, but mostly in the West Yorkshire area, by the killer who became known as The Yorkshire Ripper. A number of women, some of whom were sex workers, had been found dead with terrible mutilations, and the police were on the hunt for a maniac. The killer had already murdered ten women and had attacked and seriously injured many more when detectives received a letter and a tape-recording purporting to come from the perpetrator of the crimes. Some of the officers involved in the investigation believed from the start that the correspondence was a hoax, but the man leading the enquiry, Asst. Chief Constable George Oldfield, was convinced they were genuine. It was an electric moment when he held a news conference to announce the development, and journalists were stunned into silence when an eerie tape-recorded voice with a strong north-east accent spoke in a haunting, taunting and halting tone.

"I'm Jack. I see you're having no luck catching me. I have the greatest respect for you George, but Lord, you're no nearer catching me now than four years ago when I started."

The tape had been accompanied by a letter which was said by police to contain information which only the killer could have known.

The recorded voice sounded so distinctive that many of us were convinced that someone would recognise the speaker and he would instantly be arrested. Even if that proved not to be the case, I was aware from my studies at Newcastle University's Dept. of English Language and Literature that experts could identify the geographical origins of a particular accent to a surprisingly granular degree. If the public didn't identify him very quickly, the academics would.

We were all surprised when the next day dawned and no arrest had been made, and even more surprised when no arrest was made the day after that, and no arrest was made as weeks turned into months and the murders continued. Eventually I went to see one of my old Profs in the department who, as luck would have it, had organised and managed a comprehensive study of regional accents called The Tyneside Linguistic Survey. He confirmed that he'd been asked by the police to narrow down the area from which the man on the tape originated, and had been able to do so with amazing specificity.

"He's from one of a few streets in the Castletown area of Sunderland," he told me, "and we think he's between about 20 and 35 years old."

I was impressed. "So why haven't the police caught him?" I asked.

"I've no idea," said the Prof. "They say they've interviewed every man from the area who could possibly fall into the demographic, and have ruled them all out." (I learned later that the police claimed to have investigated and eliminated forty thousand men.)

"And would anyone who knows the man who recorded the tape definitely recognise him from his voice?" I asked.

"Think about it," said the Prof. "If the man on the tape was your dad, or your brother, or your neighbour, would you know him?" I agreed that I would, and if there was any chance at all that he was the Yorkshire Ripper, I would turn him in.

Despite all this, West Yorkshire Police continued to believe and insist that the man on the tape was the real killer. There followed several more communications from the same person, and George Oldfield kept repeating that they included details about the crimes which only the perpetrator could know. By now though, the contents of his letters to the police had been leaked, and several journalists had reported that everything in them could have been discovered by anyone who'd made a study of all the newspaper stories.

Still the murders were continuing, and eventually I called and asked if I could have ten minutes for a private meeting with George Oldfield. I was surprised when he agreed, and I went to meet him at his office in the force's headquarters in Wakefield. The veteran detective sat and listened quietly and politely as I told him the man on the tape wasn't the man they were looking for, and my reasons for saying so.

Of course I wasn't the first person to tell George Oldfield that he and his team were after the wrong man, but he remained unmoved. In a way it seemed that the detective had become flattered by the supposed killer's various hints that there was a special relationship between the two men, and that the policeman was being let down by his colleagues. The recording on the original tape ended with a segment from the 1978 song "Thank you for being a friend."

When Peter Sutcliffe was eventually arrested by a routine police patrol and confessed to the crimes, it turned out that he had been interviewed and eliminated by the enquiry team no fewer than nine times. He'd been taken off the list of suspects because his accent was from Yorkshire rather than from Wearside. He had also killed four more women in the period since police had received the tape.

More than twenty-five years later, a fragment from one of the envelopes was traced through DNA to a man called John Samuel Humble. Humble originated from the Wearside area and had been twenty-two at the time of the murders. He was sentenced to eight years in prison for perverting the course of justice.

Eventually I applied for and got a job as a producer of Granada's regional programmes. I worked on the regional news and produced some local features, and generally became comfortable with taking quick decisions in the Control Room. Among the regular presenters I worked with was the legendary Tony Wilson, who in that period was dividing his time between working in telly and being the living embodiment of a burgeoning Manchester music scene exemplified by Factory Records, The Hacienda, Joy Division, New Order, the Happy Mondays, etc. Much has been written about that time in general and Tony in particular, and it's all true. Tony was the most original, engaging, singular person I'd met up to that point. Affable and entertaining, he was far more clever and funny than anyone else around, and used to love irritating everyone by demonstrating the fact.

Tony used to drive one of those old-fashioned "Inspector Morse" Jaguar cars, and he suddenly started carrying around a huge surfboard strapped to the roof. "Why do you do that?" I asked him (I'm not even sure he'd ever gone surfing). "Oh just to piss everyone off," he replied. At another time he insisted that we should all stop referring to him as Tony; from then on he wished to be referred to as Anthony H Wilson. "Why?" I asked him. Same answer. "Because it pisses everyone off," he said, and it kinda did, except that most people laughed and said, "that's just Tony."

There can be no doubt that Tony liked to shock and make waves, and he managed to do so when he was interviewed about the recent success of Shaun Ryder and Bez from the Happy Mondays. "There's a lot of talk these days about bands having working-class roots," said Tony, "but believe me, these guys really are fucking scum." I feel sure he meant it as a compliment.

One of Tony's many mischievous pleasures was to appear to absorb any scripts or briefings ahead of important interviews, but then completely to ignore them live on air. When he'd be on the rota to present the evening news magazine programme Granada Reports, frequently he'd fail to turn up for the run-through, and then fail to turn up during the thirty seconds of opening music while the titles ran. With literally five seconds to go until the director would be obliged to cut to a shot of an empty seat, Tony would appear on camera, ready and unflustered, and proceed to conduct all elements of the show like it was his personal orchestra. He was a total TV natural and a joy to watch, and his premature death left a huge and unfillable hole.

SAMMY

—

For my first few months at Granada I commuted weekly, backwards and forwards between Newcastle and Manchester and, shortly after we moved to Heaton Moor in the 'burbs, Marilyn was pregnant with our second child. This time the delivery went much more like the textbook and with less trauma for all concerned. Our second daughter weighed in at a little over seven pounds, and we called her Claire Samantha, but with the intention from the start of calling her Sammy. She looked like "Sammy" from day one, and never looked like anyone else.

By this time Alex was just over two years old, with blonde hair and big blue-eyes. Passers-by would stop us in the street to comment on how beautiful she was. She had a lovely temperament, and was delighted to have a new baby sister. Now we had two blonde and beautiful girls. Alex still had some minor problems with what I learned were called "motor skills"; for some reason it wasn't obvious to her that the square brick should go through the square hole. We took her to all the relevant clinics and experts but no-one showed any real concern, and let us know that it was something which would mend itself over time, which it did.

Meanwhile though, from quite early on, our second child was giving us some cause for worry. Every bit as cute and happy as her older sister, Sammy wasn't gaining weight at the expected rate, and when Marilyn expressed her concern to the G.P. his response was that possibly she was allergic to the milk formula. It's amazing how easily someone desperate for reassurance can feel reassured. However over quite a few weeks and then months, Sammy was having fitful sleeps, mewling and restless as though in discomfort or pain, and still not gaining much weight. She also seemed prone to contracting coughs which persisted for longer than expected.

All this went on for some eighteen months until one day our regular G.P. was on holiday and Marilyn was seen by a female doctor we hadn't met before. They discussed Sammy's apparent slowness to gain weight, and just as she was leaving, Marilyn said "by the way, she's had a persistent cough that she hasn't been able to shift for months," at which point the new doctor called her back into the surgery, took a full history, and finally suggested that further investigations might be a good idea. She was sure there was nothing to worry about but thought we should set our minds at rest. The doctor arranged for Sammy to have a sweat test, which sounded innocuous and would be painless. A few days later, on a Thursday, we took a phone call from the hospital asking us to go in on the following Monday.

By now the growing volume of the alarm bells ringing in our heads was close to deafening and the prospect of waiting four days for an answer seemed intolerable. Our pleas for more information or even just a clue went unanswered; it was obviously not something which should be discussed on the telephone. Eventually I called our pediatrician Dr Stephen Roberts directly and told him I did not think we could stand a weekend of anxiety. He kindly took the point and agreed to see us on a Saturday morning. "Shall we bring Sammy with us?" I asked. "Yes, why don't you."

We left Alex with a neighbour and clasped Sammy close to us as we walked down the green and cream corridors of the Victorian and soon-to-close Duchess of York hospital in the suburbs of Manchester. Dr Roberts greeted us cordially and sat us down. Sammy was sitting on Marilyn's lap and playing happily with a string of beads. I tried hard to concentrate on what he was saying.

"One person in twenty-five carries the gene ... most won't ever even know it and indeed they are frequently unusually healthy ... that one person in twenty-five has to meet and have children with another of the one in twenty-five ... then one in four of their children will be unaffected ... two more in four will carry the gene harmlessly ... the fourth will have cystic fibrosis." Cystic fibrosis? I remember thinking, what the hell is that? I had a mental image of those old-fashioned children-shaped collecting boxes outside of the chemist; no, that was for (what in those days were known as) the Spastics. Or was it muscular dystrophy? I was thirty-two years old, a working journalist, an avid reader of books and newspapers, and I have to admit I could not be certain of my ability even to spell cystic fibrosis.

The rest of what the doctor had to say was semi-absorbed through a blur of emotions. "It's a disease that affects the respiratory and digestive systems. The mucus which carries the bacteria out of the lungs is thicker than it should be, so those affected are subject to lung infections." Doctor Roberts was continuing but I was anxious to get to the end. "What's the cure? How long will she be ill before she is better?" Stephen Roberts, poor man, was becoming more and more uncomfortable. "There are some very good treatments ... progress is being made all the time ... the least affected can live into their twenties ... some live only a few years ... perhaps the average is ten or twelve years." Through my instant tears I saw Marilyn hold Sammy tight to her chest and her face crumpled. "Oh no, not Sammy," she said. "She's so beautiful."

As we stumbled out of the Duchess of York hospital and collapsed in tears in each other's arms on the pavement, Marilyn and I were in a state of shock. We were confused, ill-informed and terrified of the future. One of the phrases uttered by Dr Roberts that morning was "this will change your lives." That much we could work out, but just how was a total mystery. Back home and still struggling to utter a coherent sentence, we realized some of the questions we had not asked. All this was in the days before the internet, and our wide circle of friends were almost all in the television business and at that time there were no doctors among them. So I drove into Manchester and scanned the bookshelves, only to find that medical books were too technical and family health books were too simplistic. Unable to absorb anything properly while trying to act normally in a bookshop, eventually I bought something called Practical Pediatric Problems, and in vain I searched for some words of optimism. I found a section on cystic fibrosis, and the words on the page were blurred by my tears: "The services of a surgeon may be required at several stages of the disease, e.g. for meconium ileus in the neonatal period, for lobectomy in bronchiectasis or for portocaval anastomosis if portal hypertension is severe." What on earth did it all mean? and whatever it all meant, it couldn't be about our baby. Not about Sammy, our beautiful blue-eyed kid. When would we wake up and find it was all a nightmare?

The state of breathlessness, the weight on the chest, the dull ache and frequent tears continued through the weekend. Marilyn tried to break the news gently to our families, eventually uttering the terrible words cystic fibrosis. One of those closest to us replied, "how on earth did she catch that?" It was the first time we felt as though somehow it was our fault.

I called my editor at Granada and told him I might need some time off. He did not know precisely what cystic fibrosis was either, but the tone of my voice was enough for him to realize that he needed to agree to my request.

We were asked to report back to the Duchess of York hospital on Monday morning, to be shown the first stages of precisely how our daily lives would be changed. We were directed towards a typically depressing NHS hospital waiting room with torn chairs, fading cartoons on the posters, and out of date magazines. With a grim precognition of what lay ahead, our eyes red and heavy from shedding so many tears, I remember saying to Marilyn "and so it begins."

The thick mucus not only prevents bacteria from being carried from the lungs; it also blocks the pancreas and prevents natural enzymes from reaching the stomach. CF patients are required to take enzymes with everything they eat to break down the food. If they don't, they get little benefit from anything they eat and quickly suffer from malnutrition. In the past this was the fastest cause of death among CF patients. We were shown capsules with hundreds of tiny granules inside; perhaps the capsules could be broken open and the granules spread on a spoonful of yogurt? We doubted Sam's willingness to take them.

Still more alarming was the procedure for trying to keep the thick mucus moving inside the lungs. Physiotherapy would be needed at least twice a day, every day of Sammy's life. "Percussive clapping" it was called, and it involved settling our little girl on a pillow on our laps so that her head was lower than her body, and patting her chest with cupped hands so that any mucus clinging to the walls of her lungs might get moving. Then the same on each side, and then her back. Sammy was just eighteen months old, tiny and frail. "How will she put up with that?" I asked. Marilyn's concern was even worse. "Surely she will think we are smacking her?" We were assured, though we could scarcely believe it, that our child would soon get used to the procedure. Indeed some children had been known to go to sleep while it was in progress. At least twenty minutes per session, twice a day, preceded by an inhaled nebulizer of Ventolin and followed by an inhaled nebulizer of antibiotics. Each session would end up taking a bit more than an hour. We were just beginning to see the point of the warning that "it will change your lives."

We took Sammy home with us, both Marilyn and I physically and emotionally exhausted, and we experienced all the typical reactions. I was angry with God that this had happened to our family. I felt it would be more merciful if she had been taken from us instantly. I even felt as though a faster deterioration and death would be easier to cope with. This seemed like the most cruel thing possible. Sammy would grow out of her childhood to a point where she was fully aware of her situation, she would develop her own personality, but all the time she would gradually be deteriorating. Despite my best efforts, this was what I felt in my heart. However in my head I knew that this analysis was wrong. Having Sammy for a number of years was better than not having her at all. At least she would not be impaired in such a way that she would be unable to enjoy whatever life we could make for her. Inside though, I ached. Whereas a week earlier every glance at her had brought joy, now every glance was a reminder of the heartache which she and we were facing.

By now we had contacted the Cystic Fibrosis Research Trust and spoken by telephone to a parent of a CF child. What he had to say provided some comfort and reassurance. Research into treatments was progressing well. The oldest patients were now living into their thirties. A treatment involving gene therapy was on the horizon. "The genetic problem is like a misspelled word in a volume of encyclopedias; we have to start looking for it in section A. It could be in the first few pages of the first volume, or it could be in the last volume under Z." The analogy was helpful. "When we have found the gene, the problem could be structural in which case we won't be able to do anything about it, or chemical in which case we may be able to do something." Meanwhile new and better antibiotics were being developed all the time.

All the while the nagging question in my mind and in Marilyn's was, how will Sammy die? Both of us had an unspoken dread of her fighting for breath for weeks and months on end. Of course it was the question every parent of a CF child eventually asked and, wouldn't you know it, there was no clear answer. The experience of the man from the Trust provided a little reassurance; "I knew of a case recently in which I saw a girl playing tennis on one day and three days later she had died." It's surprising what news you can find comforting when your life has been turned inside out.

Sure enough Sammy hated taking enzymes with her food and they seemed to cause her discomfort. All night long she whined, slept fitfully, and woke up crying. Exhausted from worry and stress, Marilyn and I took turns to sleep with her. In the small hours of the morning, tormented by lack of sleep, unable to do anything to discourage Sammy's continuing moan, I came close to the edge of total despair. A glance into Marilyn's eyes in the morning reflected back precisely the same exhaustion and desperation.

Eventually we settled on a type and dose of enzymes, and Sammy became used to taking them; at least eight capsules with every meal, a total of not less than thirty-six each day. For the first time her digestion seemed to be working and she gained some benefit from her frequent feeds. Slowly, gradually over weeks and months, our lives took on a kind of routine. Nebulizers, physiotherapy, enzymes, vitamins and then more nebulizers. Though the treatment was intensive and the worry was constant, Sammy was having a life. She played with her toys, began to read and write, went to children's parties, and she giggled and giggled and giggled. Her laughter was infectious and joyous. Already many of those around her could see a glimpse of the very special child she was to become.

However our routine was not to be so straightforward. From time to time, despite our best efforts, Sammy would contract a lung infection. When that happened she had to go into hospital for an intensive course of antibiotics. That was bad enough, but worse still the drugs had to be administered intravenously. We already knew that doctors trying to give Sammy inoculations had trouble finding a vein and the event was always traumatic. The antibiotics would have to be given through something called a "long line" which would need to be inserted into a vein and fed along the inside of it.

The most basic instinct shared between mankind and animals must be the one that makes us protect our young. It is the instinct which propels parents into burning houses to save their children and gives weak people the sudden strength to lift cars. Of all the traumas of those years, the worst one of all, the one that is as vivid as I write as it was on the first day it first appeared, is the look in Sammy's eyes as she pleaded with me to save her from these people who were sticking needles into her. Her screams echoed down the corridors and brought beads of sweat from experienced doctors. Her small limbs flayed with unnatural force. It took every last resource of strength and self-control to prevent me from scooping her up in my arms, dashing out of the hospital and never taking her back come what may. Whatever the consequences I will never let this child go through this again.

My own resources proved to be less than Marilyn's and the hardest parts of the burden fell on her. She was taught at an early stage how to administer intravenous antibiotics, and indeed she spent so much time in the medical bay that she was often mistaken for a doctor as she knocked air bubbles out of yet another syringe This enabled Sammy to be treated at home, where she was happiest, though it was a nightmare if a vein blocked, because it meant another trip to the hospital for another cannula to be inserted. Many times I would arrive home or at the hospital to find Marilyn and Sammy both red-eyed and traumatized. Sammy's arms were covered in bruises and in the event the long line never went in.

Later in her life when Sammy grew first into a pretty and lively child and then into a beautiful and glowing young woman, one description of her was used more than any other. People said of her that she seemed to have wisdom. It was said so often that it became a commonplace, and I believed that her wisdom came in part from having to learn early so many of the lessons which usually wait until children are much older.

When children in the playground complain that "it's not fair," that was no surprise to Sammy because she was already well used to the fact that life is not fair. Similarly we had to try to explain to her long before she was ready about the injections: why her parents who obviously loved her and wanted to protect her were allowing her to be put through pain. "I know it is awful but we have to do it to make you better." Most parents are lucky if they use the phrase to explain foul tasting cough medicine.

The frequent repetition of the antibiotics, then blood tests to measure their effectiveness, then lines becoming clogged and new ones becoming necessary, then more blood tests, all took a heavy toll. While eventually understanding the necessity for the treatment, Sammy developed a full-scale needle phobia which made her literally terrified of the injections. It made our heart sink every time we had to visit the hospital, and our stomachs churn every time she coughed more heavily than usual. The doctors even tried hypnotherapy to help her to overcome her dread, but to no avail.

Despite everything and, difficult though it may be to believe, Sammy had a wonderful childhood. She and her sister Alex formed a very close and special bond, and the knowledge of Sammy's illness made us determined to waste no time. It added an intensity to every experience. The purity of the joy that every child brings to their family was made more special because we knew it was all transitory. We took holidays in half a dozen different countries, causing curiosity and occasional consternation at customs with our huge haul of pharmaceuticals. Aged eight years old, Sammy went on an organised trip to Norway to see the real Santa. Every other kid was persuaded, but Sammy inevitably saw the stray wisp of brown hair peeping out from beneath the white wig. Already she was wise enough to say nothing to anyone but her mother. As soon as she and Alex were old enough to get a kick out of Disneyland, we went. Carrying Sammy on my shoulders to give her a grandstand view of the New Year's Eve fireworks at the Epcot Centre, her arms around my neck, her whoops of delight are deliciously vivid memories.

MEANWHILE BACK AT WORK ...

—

It was at around that time that word-processors began to replace type-writers, and I was an early adopter of an AMSTRAD, which consisted of what looked like a small portable TV and a keyboard, all attached by cables and to a micro-dot printer. Whatever you typed popped up in tiny green letters on a screen and of course it was all very primi-tive compared to what we do today, but nonetheless I thought it was rather magical. Up until this point "cut and paste" when writing TV programme scripts meant exactly that. Two secretaries in the office, Marian Woods and Barbara Cummins, would type full transcripts of our interviews, we'd mark up and then use scissors to cut out the sec-tions we wanted to include in the script, and then staple (or paste) them onto the page between paragraphs of commentary. Cut and paste.

The first word-processors were painfully slow and clunky. Everything would pause from time to time and you'd hear a whole lot of clicking and whirring as the machine saved your work onto a so-called "floppy disc" which may have been a disc but wasn't floppy. If something wasn't saved properly, or someone very close to you in your household decided to unplug your electric lead in order to plug in the vacuum cleaner, (just by way of a random example) you could lose a whole afternoon's work. Such an event could put several hours of quite severe strain on an otherwise happy marriage.

Notwithstanding what today seems its prehistoric performance, so much fun was I having with my first AMSTRAD that I started writing a story, and then continued to write a story, and before I knew it I'd written about three hundred pages of a story, which then took about a week and many replacement ribbons to print out. I packaged it up and send it to unsolicited manuscripts department at Collins, waited several weeks, and then wrote again indicating that if they didn't want to publish my novel, please would they send it back. Just a few days later I was surprised to receive a reply saying that they did indeed want to publish my novel. And they did. It was called A Power in the Land and came out in 1988 with little fanfare and to not much in the way of reviews. Still, it was exciting to have a novel published and so I set about writing another one. My second was published the following year and called The Lazarus File. It was a lovely experience to be a published author but I'm afraid I don't recommend either as your holiday reading.

My dad had done anything and everything anyone could possibly ask for our mum during her long and difficult illness, and when she died, the rest of the family naturally worried about how he would cope. Though their marriage had been far from a bed of roses, it had lasted for over thirty years and at the end they could not have been closer. However we need not have been concerned because within weeks, or more probably within days, or even possibly within hours of Mum's death, Dad had a new woman in his life. Her name was Irene, known to the world as Rene, and she'd formerly been a colleague of Dad's but was now rather more than that. Only an idiot would be prepared to believe that their relationship began after our mum's death, and whatever else my brother and I may have been, we weren't and aren't idiots.

Now this involves a sharp intake of breath. It's not easy when in the first days of grieving one's mother, to see her husband, your dad, behaving like a love-sick teenager with someone else. So difficult was it for my brother in fact, that he and Dad didn't speak for the next five years. I'm not sure that I was much happier than he was, but then I took the time to try to stand a few paces back and think it through.

During Mum's last years and months, Dad had done absolutely everything that anyone could be expected to do to take care of her. If she had known about or suspected anything about his other relationship, she showed absolutely no sign of it. My biggest concern following her death was how Dad would cope. He had always been an independent and self-reliant man, but the prospect of him being left alone in their marital home, thrown into bereavement and with our family living several hundred miles away, was all a terrible worry.

Instead of which, here he was, seeking consolation in the arms of a woman who appeared to be very nice, and also seemed ready to devote the rest of her life to taking care of him. Rene talked rather a lot, but at the time I put that down to nerves. Otherwise she was presentable, affable, apparently solvent and, most important of all, seemed to love our dad. Marilyn and I took the deep breath, then took a few more, and then welcomed Rene into our family. The two of them lived happily together for another twenty years, and she nursed him at his bedside when he eventually died aged 75. She died a year or so later, and I was grateful to her then, and still am.

WORLD IN ACTION

———

Even with everything that was going on in our home life, I was always keen to progress my career, and it was the outbreak of the Falklands war in 1982 which precipitated my eventual promotion into the World in Action team. The show was a weekly film-based current affairs programme with a unique and impressive reputation for investigative journalism. Employing twenty-two producers and researchers, and with generous production budgets, the editors could afford to deploy resources into uncovering government, legal or business wrongs at a level which would be unthinkable today. I believe it was one of the early editors, Gus McDonald, who summed up the programme's remit as being "to comfort the afflicted and to afflict the comfortable". That sounded to me like a very attractive mission statement, and it turned into a life-long vocation for a number of my contemporaries. These included intrepid journalists and investigators such as Jenny Rathbone, Tricia Lawson, Ed Vulliamy, John Smithson, David Darlow, Steve Boulton, Ian McBride, Charles Tremayne, Laurie Flynn, Michael Gillard and Simon Berthon. Especially memorable at the time was Dorothy Byrne, who went on to be the most distinguished commissioning editor of Channel 4's news and current affairs; also John Blake, who went on to become editor of the BBC Everyman series; Paul Greengrass, most of whose impressive roster of feature films fulfil the remit admirably, and that indefatigable righter of wrongs John Ware who was most recently seen making a persuasive case against former Pink Floyd musician Roger Waters for alleged antisemitism (which of course Waters denies).

Ideally organised to produce long term investigations, the series was of course hopelessly ill-equipped to cover an entirely unexpected and fast-developing war thousands of miles away in the South Atlantic. Only a few well-known TV news reporters had been allowed to go along with the Royal Navy Task Force, and so the World in Action team was left wondering what role it could usefully play, if any. Events were moving so quickly that anything recorded on film would be likely to be out of date by the time the footage and interviews had been shot, processed, edited and put on air the following Monday. The only options seemed to be to mount live studio-based presentations or debates, but there was no-one on the existing team with the appropriate skillset.

Since I'd been taking every opportunity for the previous two years to find my way onto the WIA squad, and by this time had produced a vast amount of live television, it seemed that maybe my time had come. In the event the war of course ended quickly and it wasn't until two years later that I produced several programmes about issues arising from it. But now I was thrown in and amongst the mix of hard-bitten producers and researchers, all or most of whom had done long apprenticeships in newspapers. Every one of the existing researchers was impatient to become a producer, and all had served their time digging up dirt on dodgy businessmen and corrupt cabinet ministers, former war-criminals and drug dealers. As a newcomer whose background seemed to consist mostly of daily news in regional programmes which none of them had ever seen or heard of, I think it's fair to say that I wasn't made especially welcome.

My journalistic "war stories" don't in any way compare with the genuine article as experienced by estimable reporters such as Orla Guerin, Lyse Doucet or Lindsey Hilsum, but maybe just a few of them provide some illuminating perspective on the times.

THE HEROIN BARONS

The first task I was allocated was to complete a programme which was already half-made about the campaign to site a third major national airport in the north rather than further to expand Heathrow. We called it Losing out to London and it was pretty unremarkable. My second was an investigation into how a lot of the regular villains whose standard activities were armed robbery and protection rackets had moved into importing and distributing heroin because it was a much more lucrative and less hazardous way of making a lot of money.

Most of the original journalism had been done by my friend Robert Parker who'd recently joined the WIA team from a distinguished career in print journalism. Bob arranged for us to go to see "Flash Harry" Haward, who ran nightclubs in South London and whose brother Billy had previously done six years for his part in a shooting involving the notorious Richardson brothers, and was now awaiting trial for importing a kilo of smack. Harry showed us around the manor and talked hypothetically about how hitherto straightforward "honest" villains were getting into this white powder, but that obviously this didn't include his brother. I think Harry was just curious to know more about what we were up to, and in the end wasn't happy to appear in the programme. He cut up a bit rough when we sent a camera crew to film his family going in and out of court to attend his brother's trial, and eventually he called me at my home to let me know personally that he and Billy "weren't happy". For some reason I can only guess at, and much against my usual policy at such moments, I said, "Harry, if I even trip over on the way down my garden path and have any reason to think it was anything to do with you, my mates in the Flying Squad will be raiding your nightclub every night of the week until your customers decide it's time to go elsewhere." It wasn't a total bluff, because although I didn't actually have any friends in the Flying Squad, I did have a cousin called David who was a police sergeant in Croydon. I reckoned that if the worst came to the worst David might be able to organise some irritations for Harry. Anyway it wasn't necessary because the threat seemed to be enough. "No no, don't get me wrong ..." said Harry, and I never heard from him again. Thank God.

Always anxious not to confine our journalism to London, we contacted the famous Scottish lawyer Ross Harper who was well known for representing some of the more colourful criminals in his patch. Ross was pretty colourful himself and was always keen to help the media. He told us about one of his clients who was currently in Barlinnie prison awaiting trial on a charge that he was a drug dealer who had beaten one of his gang to death with a baseball bat for injecting the heroin rather than selling it. To avoid pissing him off in the unlikely event that he's still alive, let's call him Michael McClubb. Up until recently, McClubb had pursued a consistent and dedicated career of robbery with violence, but suddenly the heroin trade was one of the few new industries which was flourishing in his part of the world, and offered greater rewards and far less risk. Unless you failed to pay your debts.

Working on the basis of "who dares wins" I asked Ross if he would consider allowing me to pose as one of his paralegals and take me into Barlinnie to meet and talk to McClubb. To my amazement

Ross agreed, and the next thing I knew I was trying to borrow a conservative suit so I could pass for a young lawyer.

I was fearful that even cursory identity checks at Barlinnie would quickly give me away, with unknown and possibly horrible consequences. But these were happy days pre-internet, and Ross's personal endorsement – a nod and a wink to the jailer - proved to be sufficient. What I didn't think it necessary to burden Ross with, was that I planned to secrete a small reel to reel tape recorder in an inside pocket, and to run the wire down my sleeve to a microphone attached to the cuff of my shirt.

Ross escorted me through all the security barriers you are familiar with from the opening titles of the sitcom Porridge; lots of jangling keys and clanging doors. Stage by stage we got deeper and further inside the hellhole that was Barlinnie. Eventually we were led into a tiny room with a table and chairs fixed to the floor. I was feeling increasingly nervous as the sound of footsteps approached, and I gently fingered the tiny switch hidden in my pocket which would start the tape.

I'd mentally prepared myself to meet a huge bruiser of a man, and was surprised when a uniformed warden came through the door, handcuffed to a small and wiry man who looked – what's the word I'm searching for? – terrifying. He looked terrifying. It's difficult to say quite what it was about him that transmitted instant and non-negotiable menace. Maybe it was the fact that he had HATE tattooed on the fingers of one hand and HATE also tattooed on the other. Or maybe it was the tattooed tear running down his cheek from the corner of one of his tiny bloodshot eyes. Or maybe it was the Mohican haircut which helpfully displayed the line of stitches tracing the shape of the rim of a pint glass atop his right ear. You get the idea. Basically he was a simple machine for producing violence.

McClubb sat down and didn't seem especially interested to meet me, and actually didn't seem all that interested to meet Ross either.

His lawyer had explained to me earlier that stacked against him was the fact that his victim's girlfriend had been present when McClubb burst into their flat and began belabouring him with a bat. Balancing the scales of justice on the other side was the fact that McClubb and his friends would be very likely to know or be able to discover the names and home addresses of any local person who found themselves on the jury. Such a person might find themselves facing a choice between a nice all-expenses paid holiday on the Costa del Sol or a rather longer stay in the high-dependency ward of the local hospital.

To come to the point, Ross introduced me as a postgraduate law student doing some research into the drugs business, and asked McGrubb if he'd mind if I asked him a few questions. He, Ross, had another client to see and would come back to collect me in half an hour or so.

Whatever else I had anticipated, I hadn't reckoned on being left alone with a man for whom severe violence came as naturally as breathing, while at the same time trying to operate a tape recorder secretly hidden about my person. As Ross left the room and I clicked on the tape, I found myself wondering whether I was more afraid of the wardens discovering the tape and throwing me into a cell, or of McClubb finding it and grinding my bones to make his bread; a feat of which I knew he would be entirely capable within the forty-five seconds it might take for any jailers within earshot to respond to a grown man screaming.

I got my recording, leaving Ross and the jailers none the wiser, and was able to play the voice of McClubb saying words to the effect of "it is the business ... buying and selling heroin ... so much better than robbing banks and stuff." Luckily no-one official ever asked how it had been possible to record a prisoner in a high-security prison cell.

THE MAN WHO LEFT HIS TRIBE

—

The whole of the UK at that time was experiencing the effects of The Troubles in Northern Ireland, but it's fair to say that the general public was sick of hearing about the matter, and it was well-known that any programme on TV covering it would be watched by risibly small audiences. The nuances of the inter-religious and various inter-factional rivalries were difficult for the general audience to get their heads around, but when the moderate Catholic MP Gerry Fitt was burned out of his own house, which had probably been set alight by more extreme members of his own side, this was something most people could relate to. I set off for my first ever visit to Belfast with my friend and colleague Eamon O'Connor, whose original home was in the province (though he didn't like it being called a province).

Though I'd seen it so often in the news, it was still a shock to be on the streets of a British city and witnessing uniformed soldiers patrolling in full battle gear and carrying mean-looking automatic weapons. Huge concrete crash barriers and checkpoints were everywhere and the whole place looked like a warzone, which of course it was. It was more in hope than expectation that we requested an interview with the leading spokesman for the IRA, Gerry Adams. Adams has insisted from that day to this that he wasn't actually a member of the IRA, but of course that was merely a semantic point.

We were very happy to be told that we could interview Adams, but not so happy to hear that it would have to take place in their offices in Dublin. Our deadline was very tight, and so we all piled into a car and headed south across the border at breakneck speed. Eventually we found the location of the Sinn Fein office, which was on a normal street but was surrounded by every kind of physical protection including huge blocks of concrete and a reinforced cage outside the door with several chambers which had to be negotiated before you could enter.

I guess in those circumstances you inevitably build up your expectations of what it's going to be like to meet a man whom you feel sure has at least witnessed and even possibly participated in violence which might range from beatings via knee-cappings to murder. Certainly these thoughts circulated around my mind when I was formulating a list of questions which would inevitably imply his complicity in burning one of his political rivals out of his home. In the event Adams proved to be formal and polite; he was dressed and groomed to appear more like a university lecturer than a blood-soaked terrorist. I felt that his eyes were cold and empty, but maybe that was just me superimposing my preconceived ideas on him. He sat down and gave the interview, and of course there was nothing I could ask him that was any more provocative or offensive than questions he had been asked many times before. He had nothing to do with Gerry Fitt, he said, and while he did not approve of what had happened to the man, he could understand why people felt sufficiently strongly about the injustices they were facing that they could turn to this kind of action. We were never going to get anywhere, and we didn't.

What did make the whole project stick in my head, however, was that it was on this assignment that I came closer to death than on any other I was involved with before or since. The situation occurred later back in Belfast when Eamon and I decided we needed to film some general scenes of the city, especially of the huge wall dividing the two communities known, ironically, as the Peace Line. Despite my having seen endless news coverage of The Troubles, the actual physical structures still came as a surprise to me, and I wanted to try to capture and convey some of the reality of it in the programme.

So it was that Eamon and I got into our car with cameraman Jon Woods and sound recordist Harry Brookes in the back, and we set off at dusk to find the best vantage points from which to record our footage. This inevitably involved us in weaving around the reinforced bases used by the army, and so at some point we must have been spotted by observers looking out for potential bombers. We were just driving slowly alongside the wall, when suddenly a large and hitherto invisible door burst open, and out ran maybe ten soldiers, all of them armed to the teeth, and who instantly surrounded the car. I had been driving, and I looked to my right to see the business end of a machine gun just a few inches away from my eye. I think I must have adjusted my focal length to see what was behind it, which was when I registered the terrified face of a kid who looked about fifteen, his lips quivering with fear, probably every bit as certain as I was that we were about to die. I actually saw his finger twitch on the trigger and had to work hard to control my natural reaction to duck my head.

To be honest I have no idea what they were shouting, but someone was shouting something very loudly, and I looked around me to see that we had guns pointing into the car from every direction. Eamon and Jon had followed the same instinct as me and had raised their hands. I looked back at the face of the young soldier and can still see it as if it was yesterday. Jesus Christ. How easily it could happen, and we'd just be a two-day story on the national news and then put down as another statistic from The Troubles. A few people would no doubt shake their heads and say, "bloody idiots - what did they think was going to happen?" and they might have been right.

In slow motion and with the most extreme care, we managed to identify ourselves to whomever was in charge, and I remember him telling us to "fuck off and don't come back." That was advice we were very ready to follow. I very willingly fucked off, edited and put out our programme called "The Man Who Left His Tribe" and never went back to Northern Ireland for another twenty years.

FOR THE BENEFIT OF MR PARRIS

———

The dominating theme of the news and current affairs in 1984 was of course the Prime Minister Mrs Thatcher and her policies for modernising Britain at any cost. Those costs included throwing three and a half million people onto the unemployment register, and drawing a line under centuries of Britain's industrial heritage. Shipyards and collieries were part of the past rather than the future, and the poor sods who'd worked in them were being left high and dry. Telling a man who'd been a steelworker or coalminer for twenty-five years that he needed to retrain as a customer service representative in a call centre was unrealistic for all but a very few.

The Conservative party under Mrs Thatcher consisted as that time of a lot of old-fashioned so-called "one nation Tories" better known at that time as "wets", and a new intake of the tougher and more dispassionate group of true believers, hewn from Thatcher granite. Among the latter was a ridiculously young MP called Matthew Parris. Parris had been the surprise choice of the candidate selection committee for West Derbyshire, alighted upon almost entirely because he'd recently dived into the Thames to save a drowning dog and, luckily for him, the chair of the committee was a dog-lover. (When I asked him later why he'd done such a stupid thing, he admitted that he'd been drunk.)

While researching different ways to cover the appalling level of unemployment, without unwittingly also producing a remedy for insomnia, an excellent researcher called Charles Tremayne read a news report of a recent speech made by Parris. In it he claimed that, at £26.80 a week, the current level of Supplementary Benefit for the unemployed was just a little bit too generous. The fact that people could just about live on it, he said, meant that they had insufficient incentive to go out to find a job. He wasn't claiming that this level of income meant you could live comfortably, but it did amount to enough, and so a bit of discomfort was necessary to persuade people to get off their arses.

It was Charles's inspired idea to challenge Matthew Parris to see if he could live for just one week on £26.80. The plan was to do our best to re-create the situation facing an unemployed man on supplementary benefit, to see how he would fare in the current jobs market.

We set about doing a bit more delving into the MP's background and discovered that he had already distinguished himself by embarrassing the Prime Minister when he was a junior assistant working in her private office. It seems that a female council tenant felt she had run out of options after complaining many times to the local authority about the disgusting state of disrepair of her council house, and in desperation had written to the Prime Minister seeking help. Instead of responding with sympathy or compassion or even a constructive suggestion, Matthew Parris's reply on behalf of Mrs Thatcher was along the lines of "you should count yourself lucky to have a council house at all rather than persistently moaning about it." The tenant took her story to The Daily Mirror, which carried a front page picture of the hapless woman sitting in her living room with walls running in damp and mould, with a copy of the letter signed by the "heartless PM". I asked the MP what had been Mrs Thatcher's reaction to his stupid mistake, and he said it had been the worst possible thing. "I'm not angry, Matthew, but I'm just so very very disappointed." Ouch.

Maybe he saw it as a way to get back into the PM's good books, but to our amazement and delight, Parris agreed to the challenge. We set about arranging lodgings in the upstairs flat of a very typical terraced house overlooking the Scotswood bridge on the edge of Newcastle. It was an area I knew well, and that our cameraman Mike Blakeley and sound recordist David Woods would have no trouble finding plenty of those grim but dramatic shots of disused shipyards, collieries and factories which would be the backdrop to our story.

At this point I'm going to start referring to the MP as Matthew, because of course we quite quickly got to know him, and to like him, and by the end of our story he had metamorphosed from quite an ugly creepy crawly into a (more or less) butterfly.

Matthew arrived at our location looking anything but the typical Tory MP. He was dressed in well-worn jeans, a donkey jacket, a pair of heavy boots, and carrying his belongings in a small holdall. He showed himself willing to get into the spirit of the experiment from the outset, as he patiently recreated his arrival in his new home for the cameras. I think we filmed in November, the flat was heated by a small gas fire, and had slot meters to pay for gas and electricity as they were used. It was dingy and depressing, but certainly there was nothing about it which was untypical for hundreds of thousands, if not millions of people in Mrs Thatcher's Britain.

We agreed with Matthew that we'd make a set of deductions from his £26.80 to represent things like insurance and cleaning materials that a person might not need to buy every week. His rent and rates would have been covered directly by the DHSS so were ignored for our purpose. Matthew insisted that he would be walking or running to and from the job centre, but agreed that most people wouldn't, and so acquiesced in some further deductions for bus fares. All this left him with something in the region of £18 to last for the seven days, which he dutifully took with him to do the weekly shop at the local supermarket.

It was always going to be easier for a single man to make the necessary compromises and sacrifices brought on by poverty than it would be for a family man, so we arranged for Matthew to be met at the supermarket by a man we'll call Frank Hamble, along with his wife and two young children. Frank had been unemployed for eighteen months, and tried to explain to Matthew that the only available jobs were part-time or so poorly paid that he couldn't afford to take them. As Matthew purchased a large haul of sausages, a tin of pilchards, and several pounds of potatoes which he'd peel, cook and mash himself, Frank explained how he and his wife would regularly miss meals altogether so that the children could eat properly.

The programme was called "For the Benefit of Mr Parris," and it's well worth watching if you can find it. It's arresting to see Matthew confronted by a group of unemployed men who tell him that it wouldn't matter if the government starved them to death; if there aren't any jobs on offer, they can't get work. One of the men, Harry Morgan, showed Matthew around the Job Centre and introduced him to his family, at which point even the MP's hitherto brittle carapace began to crumble. (In fact Matthew ended up as the best man at Harry's son's wedding.)

Needless to say, Matthew was husbanding his resources carefully. Harry and his mates invited him out one evening to the anachronistically named working men's club, where he treated himself to a pint (downed in about four seconds), then accepted another from a bloke he got chatting to, and then accepted "just a half," at which point he committed the unforgivable sin of not buying his turn. In an interview the following day he conceded that one couldn't be accepting drinks from strangers very often without buying them in return.

Plainly not easily embarrassed, Matthew was putting a few coins in the gas meter, but then going to bed early when the flame went out in order not to spend more than he had budgeted on fuel. He watched some TV, but resorted to reading by the light of a single lamp when the meter needed to be fed. As the days wore on, I confess that Charles and I were pretending to be very relaxed about counting the pennies, while all the while hoping against hope that the MP would overspend. That said, you might be able to imagine our delight when we were able to convince him that one item of entertainment in a week wasn't too much to ask for, and he decided he would go to the football match.

It's illuminating in these post-Sky days to think that entrance to St James's Park to see Newcastle United at that time cost £2.60. As I write the minimum admission price, (if you can get a ticket at all) is £32.00. Matthew went along, paid his money, and dutifully pretended to enjoy the match for our cameras.

By day six we were nearly ready to do the final count up and record the closing interview. Matthew was pretty sure that he'd got in just under the wire with a few pence to spare. Charles and I knew that he'd miscounted, and had overspent by at least a pound. In a single week. The MP began the day with a spring in his step, and as realisation of what had actually happened gradually dawned, he became more and more depressed and just a bit grumpy. In the first take of the interview he dodged and prevaricated, not quite conceding that he had failed his own test. When we cut the cameras, he asked me if I was happy.

"Not really," I said. "You didn't make the week on £26.80 and personally I think you'd come across better to admit it," and to his credit, he did. Though it probably spelled the beginning of the end of any prospect of a serious career in politics, he admitted on camera that it had all been harder than he'd anticipated, and conceded that if there were no jobs to be had, there was little point in making people suffer just for the sake of it.

Probably realising that he now had nothing to lose and that his career had just taken a massive nosedive, Matthew let me know that he'd been invited to a party later that evening in London, and since we'd got everything we needed, would it be okay for him to peel off early so he could attend? I of course said yes, and on the few occasions I have met him in the forty years since, Matthew and I have remained on good terms. He quit politics soon after in favour of a job replacing Brian Walden as presenter of Weekend World and has had a distinguished career as an author and newspaper columnist.

I was surprised when I read his autobiography to find that he impugned the integrity of the week long experiment because "the production team wanted it to end early." When next I saw him, I mentioned that his revisionist version had inadvertently defamed me, and he instantly conceded. "I think you're probably right," he said, "but I've been telling it that way for so long that I came to believe it." C'est la vie.

It's illuminating to note that the original "For the Benefit of Mr Parris" programme was watched on the night of transmission by an audience of 10.8m people, making it by far the most viewed episode in the entire history of World In Action. Did it make a jot of difference to the government's approach to the level of Supplementary Benefit for the unemployed? No.

AN APPOINTMENT WITH MR MITCHELL

—

I was soon assigned to produce another story which had been uncovered by one of our best researchers, Bob Parker. This one involved a Scotland-based dentist called James Mitchell who had apparently become very rich by carrying out massive amounts of treatment on his patients, and seemed to have a particular penchant for performing crude root canal fillings on his young female victims. In many cases he had left them with damaged nerves causing numb and partially paralysed lips and jaws, from which they would never recover. Never to be able to drink a hot drink without risk of burning or spilling. Never to be able to enjoy the sensation of a kiss. Mitchell was married to one of the famous Beverly Sisters, drove a yellow Rolls Royce with a personalised number plate, and seemed unmoved by the growing number of complaints being made by his patients.

Mitchell was already well-known in certain circles for an incident in which he'd been shot twice in the back by a former business partner over a dispute about the management of their company. The accused claimed that he'd fired in self-defence having first been shot at by Mitchell, and was found not guilty of attempted murder. Not to put too fine a point on it, James Mitchell was a total bastard.

Bob had managed to obtain all the details of the many complaints made against Mitchell, all of which made for terrible reading. Tragic though it was, it was of course a terrific story from the World in Action point of view. Most of us have been to the dentist at some time or other, and many of us have been terrified. The idea of being at the mercy of a madman who was using his instruments with all the care and compassion of a drunken roadworker with a runaway pneumatic drill would make any average viewer clench.

The most satisfactory formula for a successful World in Action in those days was to spend the first half of the programme building the case for the prosecution, and then putting the accumulated evidence to the guilty party, who then spluttered and prevaricated as best they could. In this case we were able to interview a series of victims whose stories brought tears to the eyes, then to compare James Mitchell's income and practice with other neighbouring dentists, which of course showed that he'd earned a multiple of the average income from NHS work. There was no way in a small community to keep secret the fact that we were in the area collecting these stories, and so I have no doubt that Mitchell knew about our presence long before we were finally ready to seek an interview in which he could respond to the charges against him.

There was no response to our requests. We then contacted officers from the Dental Protection Society who kindly passed on our messages and advised him to take the opportunity to present any defence he might have. Still no response. Eventually we started making plans to ambush him with a running camera so that at least we could be seen to be putting questions to him. In the business we call this "doorstepping". The problem was that Mitchell had several different surgeries in different towns, where he was able to park his Roller close enough to the door that we wouldn't get a chance to accost him without giving any warning. After a few weeks of trying to solve the problem, we let it be known in the area that we had given up and would be putting out our programme without his response. Meanwhile however, Bob had found that he worked one day a week at a surgery where he had to walk a hundred yards to his parked car. If we hid ourselves and our camera crew in a closed van and parked it between the surgery and his car, we could choose the right moment to leap out and he'd have the choice of going backwards or continuing forwards, but either way we would have him for fifty yards or so.

We waited, and we waited. It was hot and stuffy crammed into the back of the dark van, and we were beginning to wonder if somehow he had spotted us and slipped out of a back door. Then suddenly the front door of the surgery opened and out he strode, a tall and strong former Guardsman with an upright and determined gait. We waited and waited some more, and when he was close to the van, we opened the back door, burst out and started filming. He kept his cool and didn't seem to miss a beat or register obvious surprise. He just kept on walking as our cameraman started circling around him and I started asking him questions. "Can you say why there are so many complaints about your work Mr Mitchell?" "What do you have to say to the many of your patients who've suffered permanent damage from your treatment?" I can't be sure that these were the exact questions I asked him, but it didn't matter because he kept on walking as though we didn't exist.

The only point at which I thought we might get a reaction occurred when the cameraman was walking around him and his foot caught Mitchell's. There was a second when he seemed to tighten a fist and look ready to throw a punch, and I may as well admit that I was sorry he didn't. But he didn't. The programme was called "An Appointment with Mr Mitchell," and went out on ITV at the peak time of 8.30 Monday night. A few months later we learned that every one of James Mitchell's surgeries had closed and in December 1985 he was struck off the Dental Register by the General Dental Council. An away win for the team.

DRILLING FOR GOLD

Our enquiries into the payments system for NHS dentists, in which they were only rewarded when they carried out treatment but received little or nothing for problem prevention, brought some other anomalies to the attention of the intrepid Bob Parker. Conscientious dentists who spent time giving good advice to patients about dental hygiene, thereby avoiding the need for treatment, were earning far less money from the NHS than any dentist who just drilled a hole and filled it with amalgam and thereby received a fee. Prevention earned nothing, but the more treatment you did, the more you earned. A bit like financially incentivising surgeons to amputate limbs. And the more unnecessary treatment you did, the more the NHS shelled out, apparently without asking any questions about why one dentist's patients seemed to need so much more treatment than others.

This bloody stupid payments system became widely famous, with the result that the NHS experienced an influx of dentists from the other side of the world, who employed a practice which became known in the trade as "the Australian trench". It's a vivid description of a process in which, instead of carefully drilling individual holes in individual teeth and filling them, the dentist would quite literally use the drill to excavate a single trench across every tooth in each of the lower and upper jaws, and fill it with a joined up strip of amalgam. And of course the point about a dental filling is that, once it's done, (and if the clinician hasn't bothered with x-rays) there need be no evidence to show whether it had been justified or not. The result was that there were, and presumably are, thousands of people walking around with mutilated mouths, and a good many dentists living in large houses and driving flashy cars through assaulting their patients and abusing and ripping off the system.

It was against this background that our attention was drawn to two particular dentists with practices in the Midlands, whose average income from the NHS was in six-figures, which at that time was an extraordinary amount of money, and was around double the average. Since there's no point in prodding ghosts all these years later, we'll call them Randall and Hopkirk. Both lived in swanky houses, drove prestige cars with personalised number plates, and both had more complaints against them to the Family Practitioner Committee than anyone else in the region. In this case we tried and failed to get individual interviews with the two named dentists, and the resulting programme was called "Drilling for Gold".

Every one of these most sensitive programmes would have been viewed and okayed by the legal firm of Goodman Derrick, which was a left-of-centre company which had worked for Granada for many years. Whenever a hard-hitting investigation of this kind went out on air, there would be an anxious few days or weeks in which we'd wait to hear from lawyers representing whomever was the subject of the programme. When asked to give their view of our exposure with a particular show, the phrase we were always looking for was "it's a commercial risk." What does that mean? When assessing the likelihood of an action for defamation, the question the lawyers would most frequently ask about the subject at the heart of it was, "are they rich?" and if not, "do they have a professional protection service?" – someone like, (in this case) the Dental Protection Society, who might pick up the tab for a legal action. In this instance we were unconcerned about the involvement of the DPS, because our sources had tipped us off that the professional society was as appalled by the behaviour of the two dentists as we were. Their wider and ethical membership wouldn't applaud them for going to the aid of two fat-cats.

In the event, we heard nothing from either Randall or Hopkirk or their legal representatives. What we did get, to my amazement, was a very indignant threatening letter from another dentist whom we'll call Mr Albatross. At first I was confused. Who the hell was Albatross? After a few minutes I realised that we had named the old bird in a short-list of half a dozen other dentists who had earned income way in excess of the average of other NHS dentists in the region. The implication was, he alleged, that he could only have done so by performing unnecessary treatment, and that consequently his life had been ruined. He wanted an apology and substantial financial damages.

I quickly put in calls to our various sources for the story, who expressed surprise that Albatross had raised his head in such a way. He was generally known as a pompous and self-righteous fellow, but it wasn't easy to see any legitimate reason why his patients seemed to need so much more treatment than the average. Instead of being cross, he ought to have been grateful for having had so brief a mention in the show. We checked with our lawyers and sent back a carefully worded but robust "sorry you're upset but we're not going to do anything about it," response. Quite often this would be enough to make the problem go away, but in this case, it didn't. Just a short while later we received a further "letter before action" which indicated that Mr Albatross was preparing to take the matter to court. This was starting to be a nuisance.

I checked with our contact at the DPS, who confirmed that Albatross's record of complaints and lack of justifiable reason for his disproportionate treatment and income, meant that they were not prepared to back any legal action on his behalf against us. I also started making more detailed enquiries into the record of patients' complaints against him, only to discover that there were significantly more than the average, and that some of them were shockers. We approached a number of the relevant patients to see if they were willing to give evidence should the case come to court. Some were.

Like most legal actions, this one trundled on through many months and years, during which I did everything possible, short of actually contacting him directly, to dissuade Albatross from wasting his money. I know that several of his friends and colleagues advised him to let it go and get on with his life, but he was having none of it. Meanwhile I had a series of meetings with our lawyers, who engaged the eminent barristers Richard Hartley Q.C and Richard Rampton. At every stage I was assured by all concerned that our case was strong and could successfully be defended.

By the time the case was due to come to court, the journalist/researcher who had originally uncovered the story, Bob Parker, had left Granada to work for ITN. Suddenly I was holding the fort single-handed. Much of the case was very technical and detailed; I learned more than I'd ever wanted to about the alignment of the mesiobuccal cusp of the maxillary first molar with the buccal groove of the mandibular first molar, but I was on top of my subject and feeling the strength of the support of eminent lawyers.

I was unable to get much attention from Hartley and Rampton in the run up to our hearing because they were involved in what at the time became known as the "BBC versus the fascists" case, in which a group of right-wing Tory MPs were suing the Beeb for a programme which implied that their political views were far more extreme than perhaps they were. The BBC was defending itself with determination, and the case was due to last for several weeks.

I think it must have been on a Thursday that the BBC's defence collapsed without warning and the so-called fascists had won a famous victory. Suddenly our case, which had been due to be heard in a few weeks from now, was due in court next Monday. Meanwhile our barristers (who, uncharacteristically had been representing the MPs against the broadcaster) were enjoying their victory, and showing little enthusiasm for immersing themselves in the detailed technical arguments involved in the inside leg measurement of an expensive root canal treatment. A lot of work needed to be done in a short time before Monday, and they didn't seem keen to do it.

Suddenly all the legal advice which for nearly two years had been "you have a strong case and you should fight it," turned into, "hmmmm, this is looking very precarious. Coming on top of the recent defeat for the BBC, a defeat for Granada could easily lead to a massive pay out, or even a government enquiry into standards of journalism among public service broadcasters." What? We were under pressure to apologise and settle, and I had little doubt that to do so would have been the end of my journalistic career.

Early next day, on the Friday morning, I found myself being greeted in the Portland Place apartment of the lugubrious and awesome Lord Goodman. Around the breakfast table were Richard Hartley Q.C, Richard Rampton, our solicitor Patrick Swaffer, Granada's Company Secretary Alastair Mutch, the editor of World in Action Ray Fitzwalter and me. Lord Goodman sat at the head of the table, and joining us via a table-top speakerphone was the chairman of Granada, Sir Denis Forman.

Denis said nothing as Lord Goodman got under way.

"Well Denis," he said, "I've represented Granada for a very long time, and I've never before found myself in a position like this one. I have some of the most eminent counsel with us, and all of them are warning of the direst consequences …". Goodman went on for a few minutes, outlining possible outcomes which seemed to be becoming more disastrous as the seconds ticked by and the breakfast kedgeree was getting cold. Sir Denis waited until he had finished, and there was a further pause before he spoke.

"What do the programme-makers want to do?" he asked.

Goodman looked at Ray and me. Neither of us hesitated. "We want to fight."

"Well we're going to fight then," said Denis, and hung up the phone.

All the lawyers looked at each other in dismay, and as we filed out of the front door, Lord Goodman shook my hand and pulled me towards him. "You work for the best television company in the world."

"I know," I said, and it was all I could do to hold back tears, "but now we sure as hell have to win."

There followed two full days crammed with briefings and study, and we went into court on the Monday morning with a series of technical legal arguments to be decided, mostly about the admissibility of our evidence in support of the allegations. All I'd ever wanted to do was to get our case in front of a jury of ordinary people who, unlike all the lawyers, had probably visited an NHS dentist. Our side won every point, and when we returned to the court the following morning I quickly became aware of some sort of confab going on between the barristers. I spoke to Patrick Swaffer.

"What's happening?" I asked. Before he could answer, we were joined by Richard Rampton.

"The other side has folded. We've all agreed to pay our own costs."

I remember the feeling that my legs might be about to buckle under me, and I closed my eyes for several seconds, trying to absorb what had just been said. I felt a wave of gratitude towards whomever or whatever it is which seems to keep an eye on me at times of stress. When I recovered enough to speak, I saw that Hartley and Rampton had already left the court and were standing outside in the corridor, chatting and laughing. Up until that point I had been unfailingly polite and respectful, but such was the state of my emotions that restraint was not a possibility.

"So basically your advice really isn't worth shit is it?" I said.

"Oh well, you win some you lose some," they said, and tottered off down the corridor.

You win some you lose some? You win some you lose some? At this point I'd spent two years living with this case, and after the outcome of the tense negotiations over breakfast, there can be little doubt that any reputation I had was on the line. You win some you lose some? It was the renowned investigative journalist Michael Gillard who pointed out to me what should be the obvious fact that fifty per cent of the advice you get from lawyers is by definition wrong. Both sides in any case will have been advised they have a good chance of winning, otherwise they'd be unlikely to be fighting, and one of them is always going to lose. Mike himself had been the victim of exactly such a situation when he'd taken what he believed to have been the advice of a distinguished barrister that he couldn't lose if he sued Sir James Goldsmith for allegedly having defamed him. He lost his house.

Some time later I heard that Mr Albatross had given up his dental practice.

AT HOME

—

There can be little doubt that the frequent and sometimes extended foreign travel which was inevitable when working for World in Action placed a very heavy burden on my wife. Keeping Sammy in the best possible health became Marilyn's central focus, her mission in life. Preparing and persuading her to eat the most nutritious food, helping her to keep the food down so it could be digested, preparing and administering drugs delivered via a nebuliser before and after physiotherapy, the physio itself … in effect they all joined up to fill the days. Every day. Every single day. On the relatively rare occasions when both children were at school Marilyn had the occasional hour or so to herself, during which she managed to take and complete an Art foundation course, but Sammy's ever more complicated medical needs meant that her mother's hopes to continue her study had to be abandoned.

I don't think we ever said it out loud, but between us we more or less naturally edged into a routine in which I tried to compensate with our eldest daughter Alex for the attention that her mother simply didn't have enough time to give her. Our nights were still frequently disturbed, which meant that Sammy and Marilyn slept late at weekends or whenever the opportunity arose. Alex and I were both early-risers and would hang out together in the mornings, making breakfast, playing games, always trying to stay as quiet as possible so as not to disturb. We made castles out of Lego, assembled caves made of Duplo, and I built a full-sized Wendy house in the corner of our garden with a secret door at the back. We read a lot and I helped her with her schoolwork. Even at that time though, on top of everything else my wife had to contend with, I was not a good husband. No doubt my pursuit of my career was at the expense of our home life in thought and in deed, and I'm not very proud that I left most of the hardest stuff to her. I always did my best to be a good father, but overall I fear that I short-changed everyone and everything except my career.

THE SECOND COMING

I've said already that my time on World in Action enabled me to go to a lot of places I would never otherwise have visited, and to meet a lot of fascinating people I otherwise wouldn't have met.

When one of our journalists called Don Jordan came up with a story that the former actor Ronald Reagan, who was running for a second term as President of the United States, was a believer in the imminent end of the world, we wanted to know more. According to Don, Reagan had become captured by right-wing Republicans as embodied by groups like The Heritage Foundation, and then more specifically by the Christian right as exemplified by the so-called Moral Majority. Many of the more eccentric and charismatic of the televangelist preachers openly talked about the impending end of the world – known as the Rapture – in which Christ would return with a host of angels, destroying all his enemies and taking his chosen people back with him to paradise. The time was coming, and it was coming soon. The notion that the most powerful man in the world, the man with his twitchy rheumatic finger on the nuclear trigger, believed that the world was coming to an end, and with no unwelcome consequences for those who shared his religious persuasion, was potentially rather alarming. Don and I set off with reporter Mike Walsh to investigate. Once again our camera- and sound-recordists were Mike Blakeley and Phil Taylor.

We landed in Washington and picked up a few interviews with a lot of Democrats, who duly obliged us by expressing horror and alarm. For some reason I can't remember we also found ourselves interviewing the Israeli Ambassador to the USA, whose brother had been killed when trying to rescue Israeli hostages at Entebbe. Benjamin Netanyahu was impressive and charismatic, and helpfully expressed some disquiet about the possible consequences should the Saviour arrive in the anticipated fashion.

We headed into the Carolinas and visited the church of Jim and Tammy Bakker who ran something called the PTL (Praise the Lord) Network. Jim and Tammy were at that time (long before The Fall) among the most successful of those persuading their followers that the only way to defeat communism and the devil at the same time was to send dollars, lots of them, dig deep, as much as you can afford, in return for a copy of the Bible, embossed with gold lettering and bound in white skivertex. Or something. The couple lived a life of conspicuous luxury, but that was alright because God wanted his people to prosper. They never ran out of that unique mixture of preaching and screeching and smugness and whining which seemed to have won over so much of the population of the so-called Bible belt. America was blessed and Americans had been chosen by God, just so long as they were white, heterosexual, capitalist, and gave money to fight the Evil One. Who was coming. Soon.

We got to meet and interview the living legend that was Pat Boone, who was very affable and charming. Pat was very much a Reagan supporter but, unlike some others, was canny enough to play down the Presidents' adherence to some of their more out-there beliefs.

Then we were off to Lynchburg, Virginia to meet Jerry Falwell, who was the high priest of the telly-tub-thumpers. Over the years I've become a firm believer in the notion that people usually look like what they are, and Jerry was the smoothest, oiliest, most creepy, self-satisfied smug git I think I'd ever come across. Basically when he walked along, he left a trail of slime on the path behind him. If you got to shake hands with him, you felt an immediate need to take a shower. He was odious.

Nonetheless, being the devious bastards we undoubtedly were (it was the only way to be) we pretended to be open-minded and receptive to the minister's message and, maybe seeing the possibility of extending the good word and outstretched palm into Europe, he and his followers agreed to allow us access to film his televised service on the Sunday, and we would be allowed a formal sit-down interview straight afterwards. We duly made preparations to set up our camera on the balcony, and I have to think that in the course of us doing so, he must have had a word in response to enquiries made among conservatives in the UK. The word back may have been something along the lines of "Don't touch these bastards – they're left-wing radicals out to fuck you over." But by that time it was too late to throw us out, and the service was about to start. All went in line with our expectations, but when we got to the part when Jerry was preaching, he seemed to fix his gaze on us and began to speak about how Satan presented himself in many forms, and was always trying to find ways to infiltrate. It was so important, always, to be constantly vigilant against the agents of evil.

Don, Mike and I tried not to take any of this personally, especially because, after the service, we were due to do the main interview that Falwell had previously agreed to. Obviously it was important for us to maintain our pretence of being neutral observers, but nonetheless the atmosphere was a bit tense as he took his place and we turned on the lights and clapped the clapperboard.

Our recording in those days was circumscribed by the fact that film came in pre-loaded cans running for about eleven minutes, so what you didn't want to do was to run out at a crucial stage in an interview. The pause while a new magazine was being loaded was inevitably endless and awkward, and there was always the possibility that the victim would take the opportunity to regroup or even flee. So our usual technique was to start off with a lot of innocuous questions which would have the effect of putting the subject at ease, and maybe even off guard. Then we'd change to a new magazine and instantly turn on the pressure with all the evidence we had that the subject was a lying greedy scumbag (or whatever they were).

When we started up again with a new magazine of film, we immediately played Jerry Falwell a tape recording of a live broadcast he'd recently made on local radio, in which he had railed against what he described vividly as the disgusting iniquities of homosexuality, and had then given the address of a house in the neighbourhood where two gays were residents. Mike also asked him why he was asking impoverished widows to send him their last ten dollars when he was reputed to own several Cadillacs. And then we asked him if his candidate for re-election as president believed, as he apparently did, in the imminent end of the world. That sort of thing.

It was one of those occasions when being seen and heard to ask the questions was just as important as any answers, and I can't really remember what he said. What I do remember very clearly is that when we had finished and turned off the camera, you could have cut the atmosphere with a blunted loaf of unleavened communion bread. We had two reasons to be packing up our gear quickly; one was because we wanted to get out of his face as quickly as possible, and the other was that we were about to embark on a very quick drive across the Blue Ridge Mountains of Virginia if we were to catch our booked flight from Washington DC. Jerry was not as keen to be away as we were, and hung around while we packed.

"Did you read the recent story about the plane carrying executives of Playboy magazine which crashed the other day, killing all the passengers?" he asked me. I hadn't, but asked why he was mentioning it.

"God brought down that plane," he said, "to punish sinners." Since he knew we were dashing to the airport, the implication could scarcely have been more clear.

"That seems a bit harsh on the other passengers and the pilots and crew," I said. I don't think he actually used the phrase "collateral damage" but that was the gist of his reply. He gave us his little blessing, which felt very much like a little curse, and we were on our way.

We piled ourselves and our gear into a car and set off on our mercy dash north to try to catch our flight back to London. I guess we were about fifty miles into the journey, driving at around 100 mph in a 50 limit, when I became aware of a helicopter flying above us. A few moments after that I saw blue flashing lights in my mirror, pulled over, and a police officer who looked and sounded for all the world like Rod Steiger's character from "In the Heat of the Night" strolled towards us. I rolled down the window.

"License and I.D." he said.

Gingerly and slowly I fished in an inside pocket and handed him my British driving license. He looked at it for the longest while and spoke again. "D'yall have an American driving license?"

I told him I didn't, but also that I didn't think I needed one.

"Wait here," he said, and left no room for doubt when he added. "Don't go anywhere."

Catching sight of him in the driver's wing-mirror as he wobbled back to his patrol car, I was put in mind of those little men with the huge round bum and no legs that you put at the bottom of a budgerigar's cage so the bird can have fun poking it with its beak. He squeezed back into the driver's seat and I could see and half hear him speaking to someone on the radio. After a further minute or two, he rolled back alongside our car.

"You're going to have to follow me."

"Where to?"

"We're headed back to the police station at Culpeper county. You're going to have to appear in court here on Monday. We'll need to sort out your bail."

"What?"

We were indeed obliged to follow Sgt Wobblebottom back to Culpeper county, where he let us know that he'd have to summon a local magistrate to administer our bail, but that because there was an important ball-game on that afternoon, he'd be a while. Meanwhile he was obliged to put us in the cell.

He did. We waited. Then waited some more, and eventually a very everyday and reasonable looking gent of average height and weight came through the door, engaged in a discreet dialogue with the sheriff in which he seemed to be trying to talk some sense into the officer, and finally came over to the bars and told us we could go if we left a bail-bond of $200. Of course he would take it on trust that we would turn up at the court-house on Monday.

I feel pretty sure that he knew we wouldn't be turning up on Monday, but he'd already been inconvenienced enough, and so we were bailed out and allowed to get on our way. And yes, I was beginning to feel just a bit spooked.

Of course we missed our plane, but we managed to book ourselves onto the next one and I breathed a sigh of relief when the giant aircraft took off on its non-stop flight from Washington to London. At some point on the journey I fell asleep, but then in the middle of the night I was aware of waking up with an acute pain in my ears, of the type you sometimes experience when undergoing a fast and dramatic change of altitude. I think I went back to sleep, and the next thing I knew was that the plane seemed to be landing. A voice came over the speaker.

"Ladies and gentlemen, please fasten your seatbelts. We will shortly be arriving in … New York."

It transpired that we had been more than halfway to London when an explosion had incapacitated one of our engines, causing the plane to descend quickly. Since there would have been more water beneath us if we'd continued, the decision had been made to turn back. The incident had been sufficiently serious that it made the national news in the U.K. We were told we'd need to remain in New York until another plane could be located, and that might not be until the following day.

Tired and anxious, all the passengers left the plane, were shepherded onto buses and driven to a local hotel where we were told we could rest for a few hours. I lined up with everyone else and was given a key. Exhausted and more or less out of it, I took the elevator, emerged into a long dark corridor, which I walked along, looking for my room. Every doorway had a little light illuminating the number except one. Mine. I looked at the key and looked at the door. It was 666. I nearly freaked.

So now I was thinking what you must be thinking; presumably the film, when we got it back and out of processing, had been put through x-ray and was fogged and useless? No it wasn't. It was fine, and nothing else untoward happened before transmission. But blimey.

In the late 1980s, Jim Bakker resigned from the PTL ministry over a cover-up of hush money to his church secretary Jessica Hahn for an alleged rape. Subsequent revelations of accounting fraud brought about felony charges, conviction, imprisonment and divorce. Bakker later remarried and returned to televangelism, founding Morningside Church and at the last check he was hosting *The Jim Bakker Show* which focuses on the end of times and the Second Coming of Christ while promoting emergency survival products. Jerry Falwell took the opportunity of Jimmy's demise to move in and take over the PTL network, but his efforts to save it came to nought. Falwell died in 2007. Ronald Reagan won the election by a landslide, and turned out to be a popular and generally peace-making president. The episode of World in Action was entitled Ronald Reagan: the Second Coming.

THE BLACK MIST

—

I think it was my friend Bill Boyes who first suggested that we should make a World in Action programme about the Japanese Yakuza. Quite what he was thinking is beyond me, because it was obvious from the start that it going to be bloody dangerous. However the prospect of going to Japan on someone else's dollar was too tempting and so I started to immerse myself in the possible story.

It seemed that the Yakuza was and is an ancient feature of Japanese life, rooted in the samurai tradition of lonesome warriors of a Robin Hood variety, who were generally bent on righting wrongs and levelling the playing field on behalf of ordinary folk. There'd been a bit of progress since those earliest days, and now the Yakuza consisted of groups of gangsters who ran gambling, drugs, pornography and prostitution, and enforced their agenda with levels of violence which made the Japanese behaviour towards WW2 prisoners seem like a holiday camp.

These gangs were called things like Yamaguchi-gumi, and Inagawa-kai, and had very formal and rigid structures and hierarchies. Any gang member found to have committed some transgression against the Oyabun was obliged to demonstrate his contrition by cutting off one of his own fingers, and sending the severed digit to his boss in a matchbox, in which it was stored on a shelf alongside other trophies and memorabilia. We were told that this practice went back to the samurai tradition; a missing finger meant you were now less capable of keeping a firm grip on your sword; two missing fingers and you were less capable still, and so on. God knows what happened when you ran out of fingers. How would you even scratch an itch?

As part of our research we managed to obtain some news footage from NHK in Tokyo, which clearly showed three Yakuza members turning up outside the apartments of some executives of an investment company which had just gone bust, taking with it the life-savings of a lot of ordinary Japanese citizens. Apparently there had been a general feeling that the executives should have faced prosecution but, when this failed to happen, the Yakuza called the press and TV and told them to turn up at the men's homes. The footage shows the Yakuza gang smashing down the outside doors and windows of the apartment and climbing inside. We then hear a lot of spine-chilling screams of alarm and pain, and after a minute or two the Yakuza gangsters emerge the same way they went in, but are now carrying huge daggers dripping in blood. By this time the police have arrived and calmly arrest the gangsters, handcuffing and escorting them away. This was an example of the Yakuza administering justice on behalf of the ordinary people.

Aside from these endearing functions, the Yakuza also have a white-collar branch called the Sokaiya which deals in corporate crime. Members of the gangs buy a few shares in any big corporation, which then enables them to attend the firm's annual general meeting. They carefully monitor the behaviour of senior executives, particularly taking note of after-work visits to local bars, bath houses and brothels, of which there are many. A week or two before the AGM, the gangsters approach the company and threaten to stand up at the meeting and ask questions about why these executives are spending their time drinking and with loose women when they should have been working on behalf of the shareholders. Horrified by the prospect of their usual formalities and ceremonies being so rudely interrupted, the company execs pay off the Sokaiya to keep quiet. We were told that nine out of ten of the companies quoted on the Tokyo stock exchange paid off the Sokaiya, and that the practice was spreading to Japanese firms operating abroad.

The Japanese are of course well known for the imperative to maintain what roughly translates as "face", and for having a horror of washing their dirty linen in public. Nonetheless they also have an aversion to directly saying no to a request, so when we approached the police in Tokyo seeking their cooperation, they seemed to feel obliged to at least go through the motions of wanting to help us.

Ordinarily, if you go to Japan to do business and you hire a local interpreter, that person will often be working for the Japanese rather than for you. Above all, Japanese stick together, and the rest of us are mere gaijin; insufficiently intelligent and sophisticated to understand anything as subtle, sophisticated and deeply ingrained in Japanese culture as the Yakuza. However through the very smart actions of Bill Boyes, on this occasion we managed to employ the services of a very impressive young woman called Yuki. Yuki's spoken Japanese was so impressive that local people assumed she was one of them, whereas she was in fact Hong Kong Chinese so she sort of secretly hated them.

I have a vivid memory of sitting with Bill in the police station in Shinjuku where we were trying to persuade two officers to allow us to travel in the back of a patrol car as they drove through the red-light district. The police were smiling and chatting away in Japanese, and eventually Yuki turned to us, also smiling, and said:

"They are just saying 'who do these terrible gaijin think they are coming here and asking us this?' but they have told me not to tell you."

Bill and I smiled in turn and embarked on our own version of the same chattering: "Well please don't tell them that our reaction is that they can go and piss up a rope." We all continued to smile broadly, nodding our heads, and Yuki dutifully translated our words into something inoffensive. They promised to consult upwards to see what they could do for us, but we were fully aware as we left that they had no intention of doing a damned thing to assist us.

One of the Yakuza's main money-making activities was control of gambling, and it wasn't too hard for us to shoot some footage of rows of hundreds of young men dressed in dark suits and white shirts, wasting their lives and hard-earned cash by putting untold fortunes into those ghastly looking pachinko machines arranged in long lines in cavernous arcades. Another lucrative business was the sex trade, and Bill and I were obliged to recce a number of bars and clubs where similarly sad and sorry young men indulged their inexplicable urge to engage in what seemed like highly clinical and thorough gynaecological examination of naked dancers. The dancers in turn apparently felt obliged to make noises and perform gyrations indicating that they didn't really like it, which would be very understandable. We reckoned we were unlikely to get permission to film in any of these establishments, so rather than risk embarrassing the club-owners by obliging them to decline our request, we managed to sneak in a small camera and record just enough blurred images to be able to make the point, but without unintentionally becoming pornographers ourselves.

It had also been pointed out to me that one of the Yakuza traditions was to indulge in elaborate and highly artistic body tattooing, which might begin with small and relatively discreet designs on the arms and legs, but would gradually spread to cover just about every inch of flesh. Remember that these were days when tattoos were a rare sight in the UK, and when they were, they were usually tiny vignettes of homespun philosophy found embroidered into the arms of sailors or fairground workers. So once again we embarked on a quest to be allowed to film this process, and eventually found ourselves on a very fast train to Yokohama, which at the time was a far less cosmopolitan city than Tokyo, and where it appeared that they had rarely seen anyone from the west. At 6.2 in height, Bill and I were more or less freaks to be pointed out and photographed in the street. Eventually we were guided towards a suburb where the people we were about to meet, we were assured, were not Yakuza members, but since tattooing is an ancient and respected Japanese art, they were happy to let us see some of their process.

We were ushered into an upstairs room of a house which seemed to be made of paper, where we encountered two smiling men dressed only in skimpy towels around their waists, but whose bodies were covered from neck to ankles with multi-coloured tattoos. The sight of these guys was astonishing, and if that wasn't enough, they were ready and willing to be filmed as they lay down on massage tables, while the artist proceeded to fill in the colours of a line drawing of Washington Crossing the Delaware across the back of one of them. The process involved dipping an implement like a sharpened fishhook into ink and jabbing it into the skin, which then ripped the flesh as it came out, drawing more blood at every incision. The sound of tearing flesh was almost as stomach-churning as the sight. All the while the man doubling as the artist's canvas gave no indication of being in any pain, and meantime the Japanese were laughing and joking, no doubt at our expense. But I didn't mind. "Thank God," I said to myself, "we've got our film."

The main thing we were missing was any actual evidence of this horrific practice among gang members of lopping off their own fingers if they'd upset the boss. Any time we filmed in the streets in the red-light district, the muscley men outside the clubs would be standing with their arms folded and their hands tucked in beneath their elbows. Eventually, with only one day to go before we had to get on the plane, we'd run out of options and were ready to try something drastic.

Difficult though it may be to believe, each of the Yakuza gangs has offices, but of course it's definitely not okay in Japan to make a direct approach to anyone. Custom and good manners oblige you to find a third party who will introduce you, and then to approach the person, taking great care to acknowledge his status versus your own. But we now didn't have time for any of that.

We learned that the Inagawa-kai was based on an upper floor of a building which was on our way to the airport. There was no-one in the foyer when we got there, and so as we went up in the lift, I indicated to our legendary cameraman George Turner that he should carry the camera under his arm as though it wasn't in use, but run the film as the lift door was opening. It was a technique we'd used quite often before for secret filming. The resulting movie shows the lift door opening, we turn right, and suddenly there in front of us is a Japanese man who is amazed to see western visitors, and comes running towards us, shaking his hands as if to refuse in advance whatever it is we are here for. Like all good Japanese businessmen, I hand him my business card, he takes it, and I see that he has the little finger missing from his hand. I nod to George, George nods back, and we have our crucial piece of movie.

I'd imagined that the Yakuza gang might be furious at our unannounced intrusion. In the event they must have been more dismayed by the ignorance of our behaviour, which no doubt merely confirmed that we gaijin have no idea how to conduct ourselves. Obviously there was an option to throw us out, or indeed perhaps even to keep us in. Instead, and to our surprise and delight, we were introduced to the Oyabun. And far from being some brutish thug as caricatured in western-made movies, he was smartly dressed, trim and polite, and amazingly he agreed to give us an interview. Naturally we were thrilled at the idea that we'd have what might be the equivalent of a face-to-face with Al Capone. In the event the interview was courteous and indulgent, but also bland and evasive – but at least we'd got it. Was there an undertone of threat in some of what he had to say? Probably it was only in our minds.

Once back in Manchester and with the programme in the edit, I have to admit that I was more freaked out by the potential danger we'd put ourselves in than I'd been for any of the other programmes I'd made. I think that maybe the fearless audacity of the violence carried out against the executives in the investment company persuaded me that these people would be undeterred by the prospect of a similar visit to a Manchester suburb. I'm not sure what I was thinking, but I joined a gun club and took some lessons in how to handle a pistol. I went a few times, but by the time the opportunity came to buy and keep a weapon at home, my state of panic had passed.

We called the programme "The Black Mist", which is a term used in Japan as a metaphor for the ubiquitous presence of the Yakuza, and it was transmitted in our usual slot at 8.30 on a Monday evening. Once again, as always after a controversial programme, we waited for any fallout. This might have come in the form of a complaint to the regulator, or an action for defamation, or something worse. In fact what happened was that a few days after transmission, Bill and I received an invitation from the Japanese Ambassador to London. Would we kindly accompany him to lunch? We agreed to do so, and were greeted very cordially by the Ambassador and his staff and taken to a very smart and stylish Japanese restaurant a few doors from the embassy. Once inside we were shown into a private room, where we all sat cross-legged in the floor and were served the most delicious sushi and sashimi. I was really enjoying the food, but all the time I was waiting for the moment when the Ambassador would raise his concerns or complaints about the programme. What actually happened was that the conversation was kept light and general throughout; the Ambassador was delighted to hear that we had enjoyed our visit to his country, and absolutely no mention was made of the Yakuza, the Sokaiya, or the actual World in Action programme. We shook hands, bowed, went on our way, and nothing more was ever heard. I still don't completely understand any of it, but I have a feeling that somehow face was saved, we were on good terms, and it was job done.

Candidate for Union President, Newcastle University, 1970

Mum with one-year old Alex

Dad

Marilyn, in her modelling days, channelling Lauren Bacall

27th May 1975. My first appearance of BBC National news, reporting on Britain's worst ever road accident.

Cover photo for my first novel, published 1988

Sammy

A World in Action shoot: Steve Anderson,
Mike Rainer, me and David Woods

At the Royal Variety Performance, November 2001

From the title sequence of Grumpy Old Men,
featuring Arthur Smith, Rory McGrath, Tim Rice and Rick Wakeman

On location with Judith Dawson, Judy Lewis,
Alastair Campbell and Southan Morris

With my daughter Alex

Toby

Sam

Portrait of the author by "Portrait Artist of the Year" judge, Tai Shan Schierenberg

With former Chief Superintendent Parm Sandhu

With my friend Phil Manzanera

Some of the "Portrait Artist of the Year"
Production Team Nominated for a Bafta in 2024

Jen Francis, Ellie James, me, Sam Richards, David Buckley, Stephen Mangan,
Benedetta Pinelli, Joan Bakewell, Danielle Graham, Kathleen Soriano,
Southan Morris, Nelda Sale, Cora McNeill, Tai Shan Schierenberg,
Claire Pugh-Williams, Alannah Foster, Jennifer Greenwood,
Matthew McShane (hiding), James Wilkinson

A MOST UNSATISFACTORY CUSTOMER

World in Action was well known as the home of some of the toughest and most resourceful journalists anywhere, and probably the most revered and resourceful among them at that time was Michael Gillard. Michael was unlike any of the rest of us; eschewing trendy clothes or unkempt haircuts, he wore a suit and looked more like a funeral director than any kind of sleuth. Always in pursuit of shady characters up to no good and doing dodgy deals, he would stalk about the place, telling no-one what he was up to until he was good and ready. On one occasion, a new WIA producer spotted Michael drinking in a pub and nodded hello in passing. Next morning Michael sought him out and took him aside. "Never ever acknowledge me in public again," he said. "I could be working undercover." And he was completely serious. Michael worked a lot for the Observer, but even more so for Private Eye, which he and a few others like him used as much as a platform for malicious and sometimes schoolboy gossip as for legitimate journalistic investigations. However he was well connected in portals of the Establishment that few of us could even dream of penetrating, counting among his confidential sources such remote and enigmatic characters as the eccentric and notorious Tiny Rowlands of Lonrho.

I had no reason at the time to think that Michael even knew who I was, and certainly no expectation that he and I would be likely to work together. However somehow circumstances conspired so that I was asked by our editor Ray Fitzwalter to talk to him about an investigation he was pursuing into the failure of the Johnson Matthey Bank, which had gone to the wall with massive debts. The story involved a businessman and Tory supporter named Abdul Shamji, who'd built up a business and property empire called the Gomba Group. Shamji's modus operandi involved buying vast office buildings for several millions of pounds, instantly bringing in valuers who reassessed them at a much higher price, borrowing the balance to enable him to buy yet another building, revaluing that, and so on. Like most similar schemes, you could get away with this all the while you could keep moving and property prices kept going up, but the moment the market stalled, you were in trouble. It had, and he was.

At the same time Shamji was also taking advantage of whatever businesses enterprise grants and concessions were available from the Government, acquiring ailing companies at knockdown prices, and then instantly breaching the terms of the grant and stripping out the assets.

Shamji was therefore a prime target for Michael Gillard's particular expertise and style of journalism, and was made more attractive by the fact that he'd made several large donations to the Conservative party, and even hosted a dinner at his private home in Kingston-upon-Thames at which Mrs Thatcher had been among the guests.

I sat down with Michael while he told me the bones of Shamji's activities, but that the major problem was how to illustrate what was essentially a great print story so that it would be watchable and comprehensible on TV. Did I have any ideas? You need to remember that these were days before the advent of any of the sophisticated TV visuals we are used to seeing today. Our graphics designers still made the closing credits using something called Letraset, which involved a sort of transfer of individual letters one at a time by scraping them from a transparent paper sheet onto a long roll of black card, which was then put onto a machine and scrolled in front of the lens of a studio camera. Yes indeed.

I told Michael that I would take away and read his copious notes and files about Abdul Shamji, and would spend some time thinking about how to put them on the telly in a way which would make sense to the average viewer. It quickly occurred to me that what Shamji was doing was rather like building a fragile house of cards, which worked fine until someone jolted the table, at which point the whole thing tumbled spectacularly to the floor. If we could stick photographs of all of Gomba's buildings and other assets on over-sized polystyrene playing cards, maybe we could construct a visual metaphor to explain what was going on. We'd hire a lookalike actor to build the model for the cameras.

Michael listened to my idea without comment, seemed to ponder for a few minutes and then eventually said something like, "you do what you do, and I'll do what I do," which was about as close as I was going to get to an expression of approval.

Meanwhile Michael had discovered that many of Abdul Shamji's money-making scams had taken place in Nigeria, where he had agreed corrupt deals with a number of politicians and local governors. The idea was that the Gomba Group would bid for civil engineering contracts to build roads and bridges, for which payments would be made but which were never built. For example, Shamji had contracted with a regional politician who, for the sake of avoiding potential business for m'learned friends we'll call Julius Abuja, to build a four-lane highway in and out of his village near Enugu in the south-east of the country; all of which would have been fine were it not for the fact that no-one in the village owned a car. In another place Shamji's people had brought in some cement mixers and started work during the dry season on building a bridge over a river, only to discover when the rains came that the river ran elsewhere. These were terrific stories from a journalistic point of view, but absolutely no use to us because Nigeria was at the time under the rule of a strict military government which would absolutely never allow a team from British television to enter their country, let alone to film a story about corruption.

Undeterred, I heard from Michael that he was making arrangements which might enable us to enter the country under the guise of British businessmen looking for investment opportunities. We would register a new enterprise at Companies House in London, and have some suitable stationery and business cards printed. The ruse was unlikely to withstand careful or determined scrutiny, but might buy us enough time in the country for us to be able to get what we needed.

"But what about our camera and sound gear?" I asked. "Why would businessmen be carrying broadcast quality recording kit?" Michael suggested that we should break down everything into its smallest constituent parts and distribute them among our luggage. Then, if perhaps just a lens was found, we could explain that these were sample items for a potential import-export business we were considering setting up between our two countries. The final touch of our masquerade was a letter from a Nigerian based business, inviting each of us into the country to discuss commercial opportunities. "Does this company really exist?" I enquired. "Best not to ask," said Michael. Flimsy, yes, but maybe enough to get us through.

So that's exactly what we did. We arranged separate flights for ourselves and for our cameraman Lawrence Jones and sound-recordist Phil Taylor, so that we'd appear less suspicious. Eventually we arrived in Lagos and I took my place at the end of a long line of sweltering people queueing at passport control. I could see Michael on the other side of a barrier waiting for me but obviously could give no indication of recognition. As Lawrence remembers it, "I'll never forget sweating in the heat of Lagos immigration hall in my 'business suit' shirt and tie, as I bribed a Custom/immigration Officer as privately as I could with a fistful of dollars NOT to open my suitcase containing ... a dismantled Aaton Pro 16mm film camera, a zoom Lens, 3 x 400' film magazines, 3 x batteries and charger, 15 rolls of 400' colour film, and a folding photographer's tripod! My domestic Delsey suitcase weighed a ton, and I remember wheeling it about as nonchalantly as I could in the heat!"

Immigration consisted of a circular booth, the entire circumference of which was covered in dark glass, in which there were four slots where you were required to insert your passport. After an unspecified time, if you were lucky, your passport might emerge from one or other of the holes. I remember waiting, and waiting, and waiting, getting increasingly nervous at every passing minute, only to discover eventually that mine had been sitting for a while on the counter on the other side of the booth. I grabbed it, breathed a sigh of relief, and scuttled away.

Once inside the terminal, Michael indicated from a distance that we should head towards the men's room. Fortunately it was unoccupied when we got there, and we stood three urinals apart feeling relieved and relieving ourselves. "Ah," he said, "man's second greatest pleasure." It was not a thought I'd considered before, but has stayed with me ever since. And now it's going to remain with you.

Obviously there was no question of us travelling to our hotel together; we were staying overnight at some suitably anonymous international chain in Lagos, and we would meet there later. When I retrieved my suitcase and emerged onto the sultry and sweltering outside concourse, I found myself instantly surrounded by a dozen men, all of whom were shouting "taxi, taxi," and trying to grab my case out of my hand. I chose the one who seemed the most innocuous, and then quickly found myself sitting in the back of a beaten-up old car which displayed absolutely no indication that it was a cab. Soon we were hurtling in what seemed to be the general direction of downtown Lagos, and in the distance I could see a huddle of tall buildings, clustered together and thrusting upwards through a cloud of fog into a cloud of smog. The heat was almost unbearable.

It should be mentioned that evidence of the military authorities was everywhere. All the time. Uniformed soldiers carrying automatic weapons patrolled the airport, and were then to be seen travelling the roads in jeeps and other military vehicles, or were stationed in makeshift bases at any vantage point. Though the army didn't look like they might be the most disciplined in the world, they sure as hell looked as though they needed to be taken seriously.

At a certain point on the journey the traffic was becoming more dense when, with no warning, my driver turned sharp right and instantly we were travelling through narrow streets with run-down houses and derelict buildings on all sides. "Are we still heading into Lagos?" I asked. The driver nodded and said something intended to be reassuring but I had no idea what it was. What I did know was that now we were proceeding at right angles to the direction I wanted to go in.

I was probably naïve and in no danger whatever. However I remember thinking that if this chap should now swerve his vehicle into one of these derelict buildings, and I am murdered and my belongings stolen, no-one will ever know what has happened to me. I will simply have vanished, and any eventual investigation will determine that I was in the country illegally and with false papers, and therefore in some way responsible for anything untoward that had happened. I think I was reflecting on my end of days when I looked up to find that the driver was depositing me outside my hotel. He gave me my suitcase and a big beam, and I gave him a huge tip and went inside, feeling like a bloody idiot.

Once checked in and assigned rooms, it felt reassuring to be reunited with Michael and the crew. Everyone was aware that we were living slightly dangerously. We planned to fly next day to Enugu, which was where most of any evidence of Shamji's transgressions could be found. Michael had a list of sites, all of which seemed to be deep in wild terrain and far from any roads or other access. I joined a line behind perhaps a dozen people queuing at the airline ticket office. I was aware of transactions going on ahead of me, but I probably allowed my attention to wander because when I looked up fifteen minutes later, I found I was no further forward. I now started to pay attention and realised that every time a local person came to join the queue, he or she took a place ahead of me. Suddenly I had a brief but vivid glimpse into what it must have been like to be a black man in South Africa or some of the southern states of the U.S. I suppose I must have momentarily contemplated remonstrating with the perpetrators, but then common sense kicked in. It was a full two hours in the blazing sun before I was able to buy the tickets.

Every seat on the flight between Lagos and Enugu was taken, and the aisles in between were equally filled with various livestock, including several chickens and a small pig. I got chatting to the local farmer who had just bought them in a market, and by now I was beginning to cheer up a bit.

If there was a danger of us being relatively conspicuous in Lagos, we soon realised that in Enugu we were going to be a tourist attraction. Ours seemed to be the only four white faces for a hundred miles in any direction. We were booked into a local hotel, which I soon understood was both by far the most expensive I had ever stayed in, and also the worst. Everything about it was ghastly. I mean ghastly. The linen on the single bed looked as though it had never been changed; similarly the water in the swimming pool was quite literally brown. We decided that in order to minimise curiosity about our intentions, it might be best to stay out of sight, and therefore to remain in our bedrooms for the evening and overnight before we would begin filming the following day. That was when I discovered that my room was directly above the hotel's nightclub, in which every young person for miles around was dancing and cavorting to music played at an ear-splitting volume. As I lay on top of the bed, with the deep bass vibration from below making me feel like I was actually inside a huge oil drum being beaten by a maniac, my spirits began to fail. I was an illegal guest in a strange hotel deep in a country of which I knew little. I envisaged the door bursting open and half a dozen men in military uniform charging in and dragging me out into the corridor and then into the back of a truck. I'd then spend days, weeks or months imprisoned in a dark cell until the alarm might be raised, the Foreign Office asked to intervene, international diplomatic processes begun, so that possibly I might be released in three to six months, by which time I would most certainly have died of something or other. My wife would be a grieving widow, my children would be prematurely orphaned, and all for the sake of a TV show. You might say that I didn't sleep very well, and I awoke in the early hours of the next morning feeling and looking like a rat's bum. I skipped breakfast.

Michael's clandestine connections in Nigeria had enabled him to secure for us the services of a local driver and a modest-sized saloon car called a VW Jetta. Quite how we were going to get four passengers and all our gear inside presented a challenge, but where there's a will there's a way. We squeezed in. The driver seemed unwilling to converse beyond the minimum necessary to understand where we were going, but I managed to ascertain that his name was Felix. This seemed unlikely, but who wanted to argue?

Felix was at first confused when Michael explained that we wanted to head in the direction of a tiny village deep in the bush which had no access in or out other than a dirt road. We drove on tarmac for some miles before turning off onto a track, which then became narrower and darker and more overgrown as we progressed. Eventually, after what seemed like several hours but was probably only about twenty minutes, we arrived in a clearing where we came across a rusting cement mixer which looked as though it had last been used constructing the Pyramids. Alongside it was a strip of something which might once have been tarmac, but which was now a crumbling black mess covering parts of the earth beneath, and was broken up by encroaching undergrowth. Perhaps it was a hundred yards long, leading from nowhere and going nowhere. Could it ever have looked as though it was the start of a civil engineering project to build a four-lane highway? Erm, no. Could it have been enough to persuade a corrupt official who'd been paid off to witness evidence which would justify the beginning of staged payments to the contractor? Possibly.

It seemed unlikely that the otherwise ubiquitous military patrols might have reason to venture into this obscure and remote neighbourhood, but nevertheless we stopped the car and remained still for a while before we began to retrieve and assemble the various parts of the camera. I suggested to Michael that he and I should walk to the edge of the area so that we could holler a warning of any approaching vehicle, while Lawrence surveyed the scene and began filming. He walked around, taking shots from every angle, and within twenty minutes or so we had what we needed. The preposterous nature of the situation could hardly have been more clear. There could be more legitimate justification for building a major motorway on the moon than right here, and it couldn't have been more obvious that no-one seriously intended to do so. Yet Abdul Shamji had been paid many thousands of naira by the regional government, a good proportion of which had no doubt been redistributed once again to local officials.

Later that day we sought out and shot footage at a number of comparable sites; in each case there were a few abandoned and rotting construction vehicles strewn about, all of them gradually being reclaimed by the advancing jungle. Eventually we returned to the hotel and once again kept as low a profile as we could. Our only other objective on the trip was to locate and shoot film of a contract which Shamji had been awarded to build the bridge across a river which, we had been told, actually flowed some distance away from where the work had been started.

We set off again on the following day and drove on ordinary roads for about twenty miles. Felix would warn us when he saw an army patrol approaching from the other direction, and the rest of us did our best to duck down out of sight, which would have been comical had it not been so serious. Eventually, once again, we turned off the highway and proceeded along a side road which then became a dirt road and then a dirt track and eventually ended up as a lunar surface. The suspension of the VW Jetta complained loudly as Felix did his best to avoid the deepest craters.

We could scarcely believe our eyes when we arrived in a clearing to discover the rusting skeleton of an iron bridge, sitting in the middle of nowhere, and certainly nowhere near a river. Once again we were looking at compelling evidence of one of Shamji's corrupt scams. However this area felt a good deal less remote than our locations the previous day, and we knew we were taking a risk by filming in the open. Nonetheless it had to be done.

Lawrence had assembled the camera and was carrying it on his shoulder when a roar of diesel engine announced the arrival into the clearing of a military vehicle carrying an army patrol. All of us hesitated, but then I was able to whisper to Lawrence that he should act normally and continue filming. Within a few more seconds, the man I presumed was the most senior officer present was alongside me.

"What are you doing here?" His tone allowed no possibility that there could be a legitimate explanation. I took a deep breath.

"We are businessmen from England." I handed the soldier a business card. "We have been invited by your government to come to

Nigeria to consider investment opportunities. We are trying to bring new business and industry into your country."

He glanced at the business card but didn't seem interested. "Passports."

"We haven't been told we needed to carry them," I said. "Our passports are back at the hotel." All of us had our passports in our pockets and I hoped we wouldn't be searched.

"Why are you taking film?"

"We have to make a presentation to our board of directors when we get back to England," I said. "The film is a good way to show how beautiful your country is. The meeting is in London tomorrow and we are in a hurry to catch our flight." The soldier's expression indicated that possibly I was making a tiny bit of headway.

"Who gave you permission?"

"Your government. Feel free to check but meanwhile we have to be allowed to get on with our business. If we miss the flight and miss the meeting, there will be a lot of angry people in your government."

I saw him pause, but he still wasn't backing off.

"You four must come with us back to our headquarters while we check your papers."

Now I was getting seriously alarmed. "If you arrest us," I said, "there is no chance that our company will invest in new factories and jobs here, and there will be many people in your government who will be very angry indeed with you." I saw him pause again and took my chance. "Let us to return to our hotel and we will wait there while you check our story and our documents." Maybe I was managing to shake his confidence. "I promise you that you and your men will be in serious trouble with your government if you don't do as I ask."

He paused again. "Return immediately to your hotel," he said at last. "Wait there until I come for you."

"Of course, of course," I said. "We will wait."

The officer got back into his vehicle and we got back into ours. I spoke to Felix.

"We have to get the hell out of here," I said, "how can we get back to Lagos?"

"You can't," he said. "There are no internal flights today, and even if there were, by the time you got on the plane he would have alerted the airport."

"Then we have to drive," but once again Felix shook his head. "Why not?" I asked.

"Because for much of the journey there are no roads, only dirt tracks," and while I was thinking about that he added, "and we'd have to drive through the night and there are bandits along the route. They put up roadblocks and pretend to be the army and they rob and maybe kill you."

"What about driving south to Port Harcourt and seeing if we can get on a boat?"

Yet again he shook his head. "That's the first place they will look. They will block the road."

The five of us talked through the alternatives and eventually concluded that we had no choice but to set off for Lagos by road. By now it was afternoon and would soon be dark.

We piled ourselves and our gear into the Jetta and set off on a journey which started out on reasonably decent tarmac roads but then, from time to time, the surface would disappear and we would be driving over a muddy track, unable because of the huge potholes to go at more than twenty miles an hour or so. Recently I asked our cameraman Lawrence for his recollections of the ride:

"...so began a long and uncomfortable journey, through the night on some pretty atrocious roads, passing through the many various police and army checkpoints where we were warned not to travel any further as there were many 'bandits' and 'thieves' active at night on these rural routes. Every time we were waved down by flashlight and an armed uniformed police and army, the routine was the same. 'Where are you going? Where have you come from? Don't you know it's dangerous? There are bandits and thieves on these roads at night. Beware corrupt police,' (from the Army checkpoints), 'beware corrupt army,' (from the police check points,) 'Do you have any gifts for me? That is a lovely wristwatch. Is that a present for me?' This routine happened at every checkpoint and went on through the night and became very wearing to us tired occupants and we were running low on cover stories and bribe dollars. The strain and tiredness got to Mike Gillard and he finally snapped back, 'You lot are the fucking thieves and bandits!!' which was quite brave considering that the barrels of AK 47 rifles were poking in through our passenger windows."

The same sort of thing happened maybe a dozen times over the three-hundred-and-fifty-mile journey to Lagos airport. Each time we thought this must be the occasion when the men blocking the road would turn out to be robbers, and we'd be left without any possessions at best, and dead in a ditch at worst. In such circumstances, merely the need to remain polite and pay a relatively small bribe felt like a win.

The plane to London was sitting on the runway and due to take off in three hours. We realised, however, that by now the truth of our situation would have dawned, word would have been passed from Enugu to Lagos, and it was likely that soldiers would be waiting for us to check in. We said goodbye and thank you to Felix (and gave him quite a lot of money), and then I went to the ticket office.

"Are any flights due to leave for anywhere within the next two hours?"

It turned out that the only international flight leaving in time was heading for Nairobi and was going in an hour. I bought four tickets.

Michael, Lawrence, Phil and I took our seats on the aircraft, our eyes glued to the various military vehicles dashing backwards and forwards between planes on the runway. The tension mounted as our departure became due, and at any moment we expected to see a group of armed soldiers boarding our plane with the intention of dragging us off. Minutes ticked by slowly, and then the pilot announced that there would be a delay. Suddenly the doors were opened and a group of men in military fatigues came on board, looked around, and began shouting at a man at the front of the aircraft. Moments later the hapless fellow was pulled out of his seat and forced off the plane. We hardly dared to breathe, but waited again and then, after what seemed forever, the doors were closed, the plane began to taxi, and we were hurtling towards freedom. I always say that I have never seen any person go from completely sober to completely drunk as Lawrence did from the moment the wheels left the ground. The burden of twenty-four hours of suspense was suddenly lifted, and we were on our way to safety.

We had to change planes at Nairobi and couldn't get a flight out to London until the following morning. That evening we went to the hotel bar, ordered some drinks, and quickly were joined by a group of stunning looking young women, who quickly dispelled any doubt about their profession. Yes it was very hot, they pointed out, perhaps we could go back upstairs and they could help us to take a shower?

It goes without saying that we were stupid; if we hadn't been stupid we wouldn't have been in a bar in Nairobi having narrowly escaped a fate which might well have turned out to be worse than death. However none of us was quite stupid enough to acquiesce in this superficially attractive suggestion. We politely declined, but the women hadn't quite given up.

"Are you married?" said one of them to me.

"Yes, I am," I said. "Why do you ask?"

"That's good," she said.

"Why's that good?"

"It means you probably don't have AIDS."

I thought how nice it was of this kindly woman to be happy that I probably didn't have AIDS.

Safely back in London we compiled all our material and evidence and duly requested an interview with Abdul Shamji. We did not receive a reply, and after a few days we went to visit the house in the smart enclave of Coombe Hill in Kingston where he had hosted the party for Mrs Thatcher. It turned out to be a large and very expensive detached mansion in its own grounds, surrounded by high fences and locked gates. These were the days before drones made more or less anything possible, and we were irritated to discover that there was no opportunity to get a shot of the place from the surrounding roads. We waited for a few more days for a reply but none was forthcoming, so we hired a cherry-picker, temporarily blocked the narrow lane outside the Shamji house, and were able to get some film of his prestigious home.

Finally, having tried and exhausted every other means of contacting him, we resorted to lying in wait to try to do a "doorstep" interview on the run. In the event it was Michael who managed to catch Mr Shamji as he walked down the pavement on Park Lane, on his way between his office and his Roller. As Michael started to ask his questions, Shamji attacked the camera shouting "I'll break that damned thing." We had been seen to have given him the opportunity to respond to the allegations we were making, and the clip ran as a part of on-screen promotions for our series for months to follow.

There was so much good material about Abdul Shamji that the story ended up as a two-parter, called "A Most Unsatisfactory Customer" which is how he had been described by a judge looking into the failure of the Johnson Matthey Bank. I wasn't expecting a writ from Shamji and we didn't get one. However I was surprised to receive an indignant letter and demand for an apology and substantial damages from a blue-chip London based firm of lawyers representing the person we're calling Julius Abuja of Enugu. I discussed with our lawyers how to respond, and we agreed that the best thing would be to advise his firm of solicitors to ensure they had the correct current address for Mr Abuja. We thought they might be interested to know that it was a maximum-security prison in Lagos where the former politician was serving a long prison sentence for alleged corruption. We heard nothing further. Abdul Shamji was eventually sent to jail in the UK.

A VIEW FROM THE CONQUEROR

—

Altogether I produced and directed twenty-five episodes in the World in Action series over five years. Probably the most notable were the programmes I made about the controversy surrounding the sinking of the Argentine cruiser General Belgrano, thereby making inevitable an all-out shooting war in the Falklands. It's a long story but in a nutshell, after centuries of complaints and appeals to reason, Argentina had finally become fed up that the islands they knew as the Malvinas, which are 400 miles off their coast, are also known as the Falklands and belong to Britain which is 8,000 miles away. So they invaded. It happened in April 1982, at a time when three and a half million people in Britain were unemployed, and Britain's first female prime minister was more unpopular than any PM in history. The sudden invasion by what was widely seen as a tin-pot military dictatorship was a humiliation for our government, and if Mrs T had backed down or even compromised, there would have been a general election which she undoubtedly would have lost. In an emergency debate in the House of Commons called for that Saturday, Enoch Powell reminded MPs that she had recently been referred to as "the Iron Lady", but that over the forthcoming weeks, the nation would get to know of what metal she was made. As the Royal Navy Task Force steamed towards the South Atlantic, Britain imposed a two hundred mile so-called Total Exclusion Zone around the Falkland Islands, declaring that any foreign vessel found to be within it was liable to be sunk.

The British nuclear submarine Conqueror was among the first to arrive and was tasked to find the Belgrano, and they eventually found her ambling along just outside the declared Total Exclusion Zone. She was a second world war battle cruiser, was hundreds of miles away from the nearest Task Force ship, and was sailing to her home port when Conqueror was ordered to sink her; which it did, with the loss of 323 Argentinian sailors, most of them conscripts, who perished in the explosions or in the freezing waters of the South Atlantic. That meant all out war, and the rest is history.

Had the British government immediately admitted the full circumstances of the sinking of the Belgrano, there would probably have been some objections from any politicians who were against the war anyway, but little more would have been said. The headline over The Sun newspaper's account of the sinking was GOTCHA, which more or less summed up the national mood. As it was, the government decided instead to tell a string of lies about the sinking, all with the intention of giving the impression that the old tub was a bigger threat than it was, and thereby justifying the action to international opinion.

Labour MP Tam Dalyell began a campaign of asking questions and wrong-footing the government which he continued to do for weeks and months. Ministers and civil servants wondered how he seemed already to know the answers to his questions, until eventually it emerged that he was using as his source a diary which had been written by a member of the crew on board the Conqueror. Suddenly every newspaper and current affairs programme wanted to know the identity of the author. At the same time, astonished MPs were informed that a Control Room logbook from the Conqueror had gone missing. The world was divided between those who assumed it had gone missing because it contained material which further contradicted the government's account of the sinking, and others who believed it had been stolen by the same person who'd written the diary which was fuelling Dalyell's campaign to get at the truth.

At this point I benefitted from one of those pieces of luck which rarely comes your way in a life in journalism, in that Tam Dalyell, along with our mutual friend and distinguished journalist Arthur Gavshon, decided to give me the name and approximate location of the author of the diary. Specifically I received a single scrap of paper with three words handwritten on it: SETHIA – ST LUCIA. On the following day I boarded the first plane to St Lucia, tracked down a retired British Royal Navy officer called Narendra Sethia, and persuaded him to return with me to England to make a programme which we called A View from the Conqueror.

Sethia denied having stolen the logbook (and hadn't), denied having deliberately leaked his private diary (and hadn't), and made clear that he didn't think the sinking of the Belgrano was justified – not least because it was outside the TEZ and sailing home at the time it was destroyed. The show was probably the only straightforward and unambiguous scoop of my career. All very embarrassing for the government, which by now had prosecuted a senior civil servant, Clive Ponting, for having leaked documents which confirmed that the House of Commons was being misled. In the event the jury ignored a clear instruction from the judge, and Ponting was acquitted.

This was very satisfactory for those of us who preferred the truth, but none of it solved the mystery of the missing Control Room logbook. However while making the programme, someone told me the answer. It was a proper military secret relating, not to anything that happened in the Falklands War, but to the Conqueror's other and more important role in the Cold War. So I stored away all the documents in my attic, waited for nearly thirty years, and eventually wrote a book entitled Secrets of the Conqueror, which I heartily recommend to lovers of derring-do.

ONWARDS AND UPWARDS

When World in Action's distinguished series editor Ray Fitzwalter was promoted, I was asked to take over his role, which I did. I was editor for two years, during which we made many terrific and difficult programmes, not the least of which was the last in a series of campaigning shows designed to prove that the six Irish men convicted of the Birmingham bombings in 1974 were innocent and should be released from prison. Eventually they were, which was a great credit to Ian McBride and Charles Tremayne, and to the MP Chris Mullin, who between them did all the hard work. I enjoyed being editor of such a terrific and prestigious programme; we were nominated for the BAFTA in my second year as editor, and I had to work hard to maintain a stoic "the best team won it" expression when we didn't win, but this was the first of a series of promotions which began to take me away from the job of hands-on producer which I really loved.

There followed some difficult years at Granada after we successfully won renewal of the ITV franchise, but then the best TV company in the world was taken over by the Compass Group, which was primarily a catering business. The chairman Gerry Robinson was a twinkly eyed and thoroughly charming Irishman, with a streak of ruthlessness running through him like Brighton rock. His second in command was the less prepossessing but equally tough and uncompromising Charles

Allen, and the Group Finance Director was none other than Henry Staunton; the very same Henry Staunton who much later was sacked from his role as chairman of the Post Office. Far more interested in profits than programmes, and more keen to look after the interests of shareholders than of programme-makers, these men proceeded to take the best TV company in the world, turn it inside out and upside down, and to oversee the departure of many of the people who had made Granada great.

The first thing Gerry Robinson did when he took over the Granada Group was to sack the chairman of Granada Television, David Plowright. David was an iconic figure in UK broadcasting, well-known for standing up to the money men in favour of the pro-gramme-makers. It was David and his predecessor Sir Denis Forman who had been responsible for Granada's productions of some of the highest quality drama ever seen on television anywhere; Brideshead Revisited, which featured David's brother-in-law Sir Laurence Olivier, and Jewel in the Crown among many others. "Anyone in Granada who isn't a programme-maker," David used to say, "works for the programme-makers." So while in other ITV companies the Finance Director or the Sales Director or the Marketing Director were among the most senior figures, in Granada they were all deemed to be less important than the Director of Programmes. That doesn't seem eccen-tric in what was supposed to be a television company, but the mantra exemplified the attitude and outlook which made Granada unique, and everyone who worked for the company felt proud to do so.

News of the debacle arising from the Compass takeover spread into the wider world, which led former Python John Cleese to send a fax to Gerry Robinson with the helpful suggestion that he might "fuck off out of it, you ignorant, upstart caterer." It was with his equally typical panache that Gerry replied along the lines of "it seems as though I'm a bigger fan of yours than you are of mine," and inviting Cleese to lunch. Cleese went, but history doesn't tell what transpired.

On the day David Plowright was sacked, the programme-makers all signed a petition demanding his reinstatement and added his name to the closing credits of every broadcast programme. However I think that David knew that the best days of ITV were behind him and was ready to go.

I managed to stage a lucky escape from Granada as the barbarians scaled the ramparts, courtesy of the Managing Director Andrew Quinn. Andrew had been working closely with Greg Dyke, then of London Weekend Television, on plans to start independent commissioning at a new Network Centre based in London. This was the beginning of what was to be a seismic change in the way terrestrial television was run. Up until that point, the "big five" ITV companies, Granada, Yorkshire, ATV, Thames and LWT, had more or less carved up the business of producing programmes for the schedule between them. New legislation would require independent commissioning, to include at least a quarter of the schedule coming from the burgeoning independent sector which had been created primarily to service Channel 4.

It's difficult to overstate the significance of this structural change, which was achieved through some clever and determined lobbying by a small group of independent producers, who proved themselves to be more than a match for the bleating complaints of the behemoths in the existing ITV companies. Where Channel 4 had opened up opportunities for a far wider range of ideas from a far wider range of producers, the bigger budgets and larger audiences available via the ITV schedule would be a game-changer.

As the form of the new ITV Network Centre began to evolve, no doubt the usual inter-company politics were immediately coming into play, and speculation was rife on the subject of who would be the new Managing Director of ITV, who would be the first Director of Programmes, who would be the first Commissioning Editors etc.

Among those most desperate to get the job of Network Director was Granada's Director of Programmes Steve Morrison. Steve was energetic and able, but also had a reputation for being a bit devious, so probably would not have been a popular choice. What would always have been an unlikely appointment became even more unlikely when it was announced that Andrew Quinn himself had been persuaded to become the first MD of the new ITV. Certainly it was unthinkable that the first two key appointments could both come from Granada, and indeed the usual politics delivered the first Network Director from London Weekend Television. Marcus Plantin had a great reputation as Head of Light Entertainment, though he freely admitted that he knew little about drama and next to nothing about factual programmes.

I'd worked closely with Andrew Quinn on various aspects of the recent ITV franchise round, and so was delighted when word reached me that he'd kindly suggested me as the Controller of ITV's Factual programmes. The role would include looking after the channel's news, current affairs, factual entertainment, arts, documentaries and religion. (Finally my A level in Divinity would come into its own.) It would mean a move to the new headquarters at the former Sunday Times building in Gray's Inn Road, but with so much change and instability at Granada, it was a relatively easy decision to make.

In 1993 I started a whole new life of commuting on Sunday nights and Friday nights between our home in Manchester and a rented flat in London. My immediate colleagues were Vernon Lawrence, late of Yorkshire TV, who was commissioning drama and entertainment, and Dawn Airey from Central TV who was appointed to run Children's and Daytime programmes. Both were lovely colleagues, and I remember that Dawn in particular took a conscientious interest in everything to do with ratings and scheduling, which no doubt stood her in good stead when later she went on to run Channel 5.

My life of isolation in a tiny flat just a few yards along the road from the office meant that I could work long hours wading through every programme proposal from every independent production company, the vast majority of which had been originally developed for, and rejected by, Channel 4. There were literally hundreds of them, but I had only a few factual slots to allocate each week, and so I had no alternative but to reject ninety-nine for every one I was able to encourage.

ITV's factual programmes at that time were a haphazard mess, with no consistency, strategy, or brand. Even the news was branded ITN rather than ITV, and when I asked why ours was the only television channel in the world which wasn't allowed to call its news service the same name as the channel, senior executives at the news provider stopped talking to me. (I eventually got my way, hence today's ITV News.)

The few existing documentary slots had been more or less carved up between Central Television (in the Midlands), Yorkshire, and Granada. Each of them had established their own strand names, perhaps the most famous of which was Yorkshire's "First Tuesday', so called because it was transmitted on the first Tuesday of each month. What that meant, aside from anything else, was that ITV could never transmit a four-part documentary series without running into a First Tuesday slot.

I faced a storm of opposition when I insisted that we were scrapping all the existing titles, and commissioning individual documentaries on their merit from whichever ITV or independent company had the best ideas. They'd all play under a new regular weekly umbrella title called Network First. We did, and in its first year on air, the Network First series included a report from East Timor by the indefatigable John Pilger entitled "Death of a Nation", a film by Peter Gordon from Yorkshire TV entitled "Children of the Holocaust" and a behind the scenes access film with the London School of Ballet. The series won The Royal Television Society award for Best Factual Series.

I was lucky that Marcus Plantin had sufficient confidence in his chosen team to delegate most of the decision-making. Unlike the majority of commissioning editors today, I was given a set of designated slots and a budget, and told to commission more or less whatever I wanted. Marcus wanted the final sign off, but generally his attitude was, "I don't know much about factual programmes, but you do, so that's alright." A rare breed even then, and an endangered species now. Marcus sadly died in 2023.

I loved working with great documentary makers like Phillip Whitehead on series such as The Windsors and with Melvyn Bragg on the South Bank Show. I remember the great producer/director Anthony Summers regaling me with all his well-known passion about a film he wanted to make about all the contradictions involved in mankind's relationship with different animals – contrasting behaviours from pet parlours in Hollywood to cooking and eating cats in Korea. His remarkable film entitled Man and Animals was transmitted in November 1985.

More out of curiosity than anything, I agreed to a meeting with Prince Edward who at that time was trying to get into the television industry. I commissioned his company, Ardent Productions, to make a one-off called "Edward on Edward" in the course of which I had to persuade the young Prince that the audience was unlikely to share the sympathy he felt for his uncle for finding himself having to sponge off the goodwill of rich Americans who relished the idea of having "a Dook" to dinner. It ended up as quite a nice film, but I'm afraid that Ardent didn't last very long.

I was also asked to join the Advisory Board of the charity Victim Support, and regularly attended meetings chaired by Princess Anne, whom I found to be unfailingly hard-working, conscientious, and completely without pomposity or self-importance.

Among my favourite things to do was to work with David Frost on everything from "Beyond Belief" which investigated the supernatural, to Guinness World Records. It became a regular monthly treat to have lunch with David, usually at his favourite haunt at Langan's Brasserie. One day, and uncharacteristically, he arrived late and was full of apologies. He explained that just as he was leaving the office, he'd received a call from a newspaper informing him that his friend Peter Cook had died, and asking for a tribute.

"And what did you say?" I asked him.

"I said that when I met Peter Cook, it was the first time I was aware that I was in the presence of a genius." David paused for effect and then added. "And the second time was when I met Stuart Prebble, but will they print that?" David was quite literally unique and the world is a far less colourful place without him.

LOSS

—

Marilyn was understandably reluctant to lose the support structure she had among the medical community in Manchester, and to leave our network of close friends. The children were also less than thrilled at the prospect of moving to London. However six months of commuting at weekends was enough to convince us all that the move was the lesser of evils, and eventually things worked out well. The girls settled quickly and happily into Ibstock Place school at Roehampton, and we moved into a house in Coombe Hill in Kingston (which, coincidentally, was just around the corner from Abdul Shamji.) Still, we had all had a tough year and, despite some financial pressures, we decided to go back to Florida for Christmas. This time we had to freight ahead dozens of bottles of high-calorie night-time feed, which would be delivered directly into Sammy's tummy through a new and surgically-installed gastrostomy. We nailed the drip feed to the wall beside her hotel room bed. Once again we watched spectacular New Year's Eve fireworks at Disneyland, and that night was one of many that she went to sleep during her physiotherapy.

Alex progressed well at her new school and had a lovely relationship with her younger sister. They were sufficiently close in age to enjoy the same games at the same time; they spent countless hours playing together, and could scarcely be persuaded to come downstairs for meals if they were about to break into a new level in whatever was the latest computer game. Each hard-won breakthrough was accompanied by unconstrained shrieks of delight.

Sammy learned to play the piano, was a gifted artist, made wonderful friends, and worked hard at school. Now she was under the care of the magnificent Brompton Hospital in Chelsea, where she would sometimes need to stay for a course of antibiotics aimed at staving off infections. It was a moment of great pride for everyone when she was allowed out of the Brompton for a day to receive a class prize from "Nightshade" from the TV show "The Gladiators".

Mostly though, she was quick, clever and funny. Sometimes she would come home troubled because one of the boys who did not know of her problem had made fun of her less than average height. She would work on an effective put down line, and more often than not she would return home next day triumphant. She learned the power of words and wit and used them to great effect. Videos of family holidays show Sammy constantly making faces, moving into shot, monopolising the lens. She performed sketches, recited her favorite speeches from Blackadder, made up songs. Wherever Sammy went, the light seemed to follow her.

It was in that summer, when Sammy was thirteen, that her condition began to cause serious concern. Her lung X-rays were not clear and her cough persisted even after the usual two week stay in hospital. She began to feel depressed and was losing weight. Doctors decided to keep her for a third week in the hope of kicking the problem before we took a summer holiday at a house we had rented at Gurnard Bay on the Isle of Wight. Not convinced that she was in the clear, the medical team thought the holiday would bring her more benefit than a further extension of her treatment. We steered our way through the mountain of bureaucracy which was necessary in order to have oxygen cylinders installed in our holiday home. Though weakened by the long stay in hospital and now using a wheelchair for anything more than the shortest walk, we had a wonderful time, and Sammy slept well and enjoyed sitting in the sun.

At the end of the summer however, her weight was still slipping. When all her friends went back to school, Sammy went back into hospital. This time the antibiotics were being changed every few days, and the doctor seemed less certain of their course of action. Their concern about her falling weight was mounting, and she was being urged to take high-calorie drinks by day as well as by night. She did her best but found them ghastly. After a drink she would sit on her bed for the longest time trying to prevent herself from throwing up. As often as not she failed, and the whole exercise had been wasted.

As Christmas approached, Marilyn and I were keen that both sets of grandparents should join us at home. Though neither of us said it aloud, we both feared that this might be the last that we would all be together. The home video shows Sammy ripping open her presents with as much enthusiasm as ever, displaying plausible gratitude for things she did not really want, kissing grandparents, and laughing infectiously as I modelled my traditional Christmas pair of eccentric socks. She ate very little lunch and had hardly any energy. Her diary for New Year's Eve reads, "I hope next year is better than this one has been."

Sammy was now too weak to attend school and would go in once or twice a week to do some art. Her friends remained close and in touch, but often she did not feel too much like hearing about all the things they had been doing. Parties and cinema visits and boyfriends that she was missing out on.

Her weight loss was giving increasing cause for concern and led to another stay in hospital. Investigations suggested that Sammy was suffering from diabetes, which is a common side effect of cystic fibrosis. We were told that she would have to face injections every day. By now her morale was already low and at first Sammy refused. She would do anything, anything, rather than face such a prospect. The decision was postponed but three more weeks of intensive hospital treatment produced little sign of improvement. At the end of the three weeks, Marilyn and I were called to a meeting with her Consultant Dr. Andrew Bush.

The subject of heart and lung transplants had been raised before but only in very general terms. It was not something doctors urged people to think about unless and until they were close to the end of other alternatives. That point had now been reached with Sammy and Dr. Bush wanted us all to think carefully about putting her on the waiting list.

It would mean that Sammy would be required to undergo many tests and would have to remain under intensive treatment to give her the best possible chance. She would be unlikely to be allowed out of hospital, and if she was allowed out she would carry a bleep at all times. If the bleep went off she would have to be rushed to hospital directly. Even if a suitable donor was found in the right time, the problems were by no means over. A proportion of patients do not survive the operation. Even if it is successful, it's followed by an intensive regime of anti-rejection drugs. At the end of three years half of all heart lung transplant patients were still alive. Beyond that would still be uncertain.

Although we knew it in our hearts, the news that the situation had become so desperate was still a shock. Marilyn and I knew that in her current morale, Sammy's reaction to the proposition of a transplant would be swift and negative. We asked to take her home for a few days in order to give her a better chance to think clearly. Until recently we had taken most of her medical decisions for her, but it was now clear that she was determined to take them herself.

That evening we sat down with her and talked through the options. Though Sammy had known for a long time that her prospects were grim, this brought her situation into sharp focus. For the first time in all the years of her illness, I was unable to keep self-control in front of her as I told her the situation. My own tears no doubt added to her sense of shock. She cried bitterly and we all cried together. Doing the very best I could to remain rational, I described the alternatives as dispassionately as I could. Whatever she wanted to do would be the right decision; Marilyn and I would back her all the way. We did not want Sammy to answer immediately. She needed to give herself time to absorb the position and to make her choices. She agreed to do so but both Marilyn and I already knew her answer.

Several days later Sammy told us that she would rather spend whatever time she had left at home with the three of us and with her beloved cat. Agonizing though it was, we knew that for her this was the right decision. Had there been any realistic prospect of a long-term successful outcome, no doubt we would all have pursued it as far as it was possible to go, but the transplant route had been described to us as "swapping one illness for another" at best, with enormous risks and trauma along the way. Sammy felt that she had endured enough already, and neither Marilyn nor I could confidently try to contradict her.

Now Sammy stayed at home with Marilyn and we started to get help from the Paediatric Outreach Nursing Team (PONT) from Kingston hospital. Liz, Jane and Penny were to become very special friends to all of us in the weeks ahead. These were golden days, bonus hours, treasured memories. Every moment was special and precious because we all knew that time was slipping away. Sometimes Sammy discussed her situation very frankly with Marilyn; with me she preferred to keep up something closer to normality.

Back at home and gradually becoming weaker, Sammy eventually intimated to Marilyn that she wanted to discuss her situation with me. I doubted my own ability to get through a frank conversation with my daughter about her impending death, but I knew I had to find the strength from somewhere to do it. One evening I sat on the sofa with her in my arms.

I told our daughter what little I knew about death. I had recently commissioned a documentary about near-death experiences in which everyone told a similar story. They felt themselves to be dreaming, and then saw a bright light. The light was warm and welcoming and they heard their names being called. At that moment they felt as though there was nothing they wanted to do more than to go towards that light and towards that welcoming voice. There was no fear and no sadness.

"Are you afraid?"

"Sometimes."

I told her that the main regret felt by my mother who had died prematurely fifteen years before was that she had missed seeing Sammy come into the world. She was a wonderful woman who would be waiting to welcome her granddaughter to wherever she was going. Sammy's beloved cat Widgie, who had died a year before, would also be waiting. We talked about how much we would all miss Sammy, but that I felt she would be with us every day and that one day we would all be together. Sammy cried, and I cried, and in the end she was stronger than me, telling me that with enough love we would all come through it.

After that evening we spoke about her situation many times. She was disappointed that there was no answer to the question "why me?" but not embittered or debilitated by it. Her main concerns were that Marilyn, Alex and I should promise two things; one, that the three of us would eventually resume a normal life after she left us, and secondly that we would be sure to take good care of her pet cat Magic. More confident of the second than the first, we were glad to give both undertakings.

On Saturday 17th of August, Sammy wanted to buy some model cats which had caught her eye, and Alex and I took her to the local shops to get them. She was delighted to have got what she wanted and happily placed them beside her bed. That evening I took her for a long walk in her wheelchair, and we talked of many things. She was calm and strong and full of wisdom. I told her again that we would never forget her and that one day we would all be together again. Her breathing had begun to be more difficult at night, and for the first time she was given something to suppress her cough and give her a more restful sleep.

On Sunday the 18th Sammy woke up early and Marilyn and I took turns to sit beside her bed while she rested and talked some more. Eventually she returned to sleep and when she woke up again mid-morning, her hands and feet felt cold. Penny from the PONT team visited us and suggested we call Dr. Wilson. Dr. Wilson was and is a wonderful man who had talked frankly and openly to us and to Sammy about her situation. He assured us all, and we believed him, that she would suffer no distress at the end. As he left us on that morning, he told us that Sammy was running out of time.

That Sunday Marilyn, Alex and I spent the day sitting beside Sammy in her bedroom. Sometimes she was dozing but often she would wake up and look around her. When she did so, one of us was holding her hand and telling her how much we loved her. Several times she said how wonderful it was to wake up and find a room filled with so much love, and that she was having a lovely day. She also said that when she closed her eyes she felt that she was in paradise.

That evening Sammy's sister Alex kissed her goodnight and told her that she loved her. At around 11 o'clock Sammy went peacefully to sleep, and Marilyn and I decided to take shifts in sitting with her. There seemed to be no imminent crisis so I would take over at 4am. My next conscious moment was when Marilyn came into the room and asked me to help her.

She and I both sat beside Sammy on her bed, and at one moment she was with us and the next moment she was gone. She left us in the most peaceful way, and her beautiful and extraordinary spirit was free.

Claire Samantha Prebble was a lot of presence for a little girl.

She touched a great many people and illuminated a great many lives. Letters of condolences spoke of fun, wit, infectious laughter, consideration for others and lots of love. On the day before Sammy's funeral Alex learned that she had passed seven out of her eight GCSEs which, in the circumstances, was a minor miracle.

The service was conducted by an old friend from Newcastle, Geoff Smith, who is an Anglican Minister. The chapel was packed with family, friends, teachers, doctors and nurses, and as they left the service each one placed a single flower on her coffin. It was Geoff who suggested "Perfect Day" by Lou Reed as the final piece of music, but only much later that I wondered about the significance of the closing lyric. "You're going to reap just what you sew." Well, maybe.

The weeks after Sammy died were something like walking through a strange country, in which much of what you see about you is familiar, but every time you turn a corner you find yourself feeling detached and confused, and in alien territory. You know you are at home, but you don't quite recognize the world you're living in. The first time you find yourself setting the table for a meal and setting three places rather than four. The first time three of you all get into the car and fasten seat belts, but one of you is missing. The first time anyone asks you how many children you have.

First in our list of priorities was how Alex would cope with the pain and loss of her beloved sister, and I know that several well-meaning people urged her to take some time off, maybe a year, and resume her education later. I was grateful when her immediate reaction was that she wanted none of that, and felt strongly that Sammy would want her to get on with her own life. She enrolled in a course studying Health and Social Policy at Esher College and threw herself into her new environment. We three remaining members of our immediate family shared our tears and eventually our smiles and our laughter, but no-one gets out of these things unscathed, and Alex of course had her own issues arising from the experience of losing her closest friend and sibling. She waited for many years before seeking professional bereavement counselling, but eventually was glad that she did and would thoroughly recommend it to anyone in a similar situation.

It's hard for me to know what to say about how Marilyn dealt with things at the time. We held each other tight in all senses, and tried to navigate these strange and unfamiliar feelings together. Often we simply cried. Very often. But then sometimes a photo or a memory would trigger a funny memory, and we would laugh and cry at the same time. We felt the love and support of friends and family, but mostly people had no idea what to say to us, and usually what they did say was well meant but foolish.

"I know how you feel – my mother died last year. Mind you, she was eighty."

Very little of what was said with good intentions resonated, but it was Dr Richard Wilson, who had helped us to care for Sammy in her last weeks, who came closest to getting it right.

"It's like losing a limb," he told us, "you eventually learn to cope and to live a life which is near to normal, but you've never not lost a limb." That's about it. Sometimes the day is clear and the sun is shining, but there's never not a bloody big piece of the jigsaw missing from the blue sky. Life is never ever the same, but you don't want it to be the same, because that loss is a precious part of our lives.

I returned to work within a fortnight of Sammy's death, which was probably too soon and a mistake, but I felt a strong urge to distract myself by getting on with something. At the time we were living in Kingston and my morning drive to work on the South Bank never took less than ninety minutes. Each day on the journey I would deliberately allow my mind the freedom to wander over all the things that had happened, and every day for two years I cried. Nothing could stop me. Every single day for two years, on that journey or at some other moment on weekends, I would find that the tears would be streaming down my face, and sometimes I would find myself wailing out loud for the loss of our child. After all that time, just gradually, the tears began to be less frequent, but we've kept our promise to Sammy that we would think about her every day of our lives, and today, more than twenty-five years after all this happened, I am still never more than five seconds away from tears.

ITV

All this happened at a time of fast change in the TV industry, which was quickly being dragged from the cosy duopoly of a strong publicly funded BBC competing with a strong advertiser funded ITV. Someone once said that a monopoly is a terrible thing unless you happen to own one, and for the first twenty-seven years of its existence, ITV had a monopoly of advertising on television. And like most if not eventually all monopolies, it was abused. It was abused by the trade unions, who used the companies' imperative to stay on air at all costs to drive through rates of pay and working practices which were indefensible by any normal standards. And it was abused by the companies themselves who treated the advertisers very badly, often forcing them into deals they didn't want with a "take it or leave it" attitude which was only possible because there was nowhere else to go.

It's interesting to note that the Bernstein family which had owned and run the original Granada chain of cinemas had at first opposed the introduction of commercial television and then, when it became inevitable, applied for and won the ITV franchise for the north west of England. Then when Channel 4 was first mooted, the ITV companies resisted it with all their strength but when it also became inevitable, they sought to manage and sell its airtime. Now coming along was TV delivered by satellite and, finding that it could not be resisted, ITV wanted to get on board. The earliest debacle involving the brief and bloody contest between Rupert Murdoch's Sky and British Satellite Broadcasting's "Squarial" has been widely documented and did not end well for the terrestrial broadcasters. By the time I became involved, Sky was well established and Granada wanted a piece of the action.

At that time Sky was desperately searching for content to populate its burgeoning package of new channels being delivered by satellite, and Granada was seeing the train leaving the station and keen to roll along. So they teamed up together to launch something imaginatively called Granada Sky Broadcasting (GSB) and asked me to become the CEO.

This was to be my next big move from being close to pro-gramme-making to the world of suits, and I felt apprehensive and slightly out of my depth, but also excited and enthused. I quickly realised that I'd have to become far more business-literate than had hitherto been necessary, so I took myself along to the bookshop and bought an armful of teach yourself-type volumes. "How to read the financial pages," "How to read a balance sheet," stuff like that. I had to concentrate hard, but soon found myself more or less understanding what Rob Ovens (the Finance Director) was telling me.

We started up a little suite of digital channels which played on an obscure offshoot of the main Sky satellite, and we needed to negoti-ate agreements for their carriage on the various cable systems which were then part of the fast-changing programme delivery networks. Telewest, Cable and Wireless etc had dreadful reputations for customer service, but were delivering multi-channels into households and would pay a few pence per subscriber per month for the privilege of doing so.

Our original channels were called Granada Plus, which sched-uled repeats from Granada's archives going back over several decades; Granada Good Life, for which Granada invented a whole new econ-omy of mass programme making, and in the course of which they discovered talents like Trinny and Susannah. We also had Talk TV, which was all chat, and where we discovered and broadcast a very unusual and original young man called Sacha Baron-Cohen.

To say that these new channels were marginal to the mainstream of broadcasting is an understatement. Given the limited distribution on new platforms which were offering services such as Nickelodeon and UK Gold, we were always going to struggle to achieve much visibility. The traditional measurement of success in doing so, which also provided the data on which advertising revenue was based, was called the Broadcasters' Audience Research Board. BARB operated through set-top boxes installed in a sample of households throughout the country, which sent back information on viewing habits across the various demographics. But BARB had of course been set up to service the existing terrestrial channels which at that time had audiences in the millions, and its sample size was lamentably unsuited to measuring relatively tiny numbers of viewers. Nonetheless, each day we would eagerly await and then hungrily scan rows of figures and decimals to see if our audiences had registered. Sadly, more often than not, we were looking at rows of 0.0 or, if we were lucky, 0.1. 0.1, we were told, meant that we might have an audience of ten thousand people watching our shows, which was of course pathetic, but in any event felt like progress.

When the first three months passed by and it came to deciding which programmes in our schedule we should continue with, and which we should cancel, the one reliable and regular performer was "Rosemary Conley's Workout", which is a Ronseal title requiring no further explanation. However the show had a consistent BARB rating of 0.1, and in times of extreme drought, even a drop of rain is welcome; therefore we recommissioned a new series from Rosemary.

Then, would you believe it, suddenly our reliable audience for Rosemary of 0.1. vanished and we started to see rows of 0.0. Our supposed ten thousand viewers had disappeared without trace. It's difficult to overstate what a blow this was and, now at my wits' end and in some desperation, I called the head of BARB and asked for an investigation. How could a regular and reliable audience of at least ten thousand people suddenly evaporate? I forget her name now, but a very nice woman undertook to make enquiries and get back to me. A few days later she did. Purely by chance, it turned out, Rosemary Conley's niece had a BARB set-top box in her home, and had gone away on holiday and so was not watching the telly. Hence our audience measured at ten thousand had vanished with her. No doubt "normal service" would be resumed as soon as she returned home and began watching her aunt's exercise class. She did, and we got our regular measurement of 0.1 back.

All my TV background up until this stage had been at the BBC and ITV, and so my education into the world of multi-channels was coming thick and fast. You could probably imagine just how happy I was when I learned that the well-known TV astrologer Russell Grant had pre-recorded six months' worth of daily horoscopes for the Granada Good Life channel, and that inadvertently the team had been transmitting them in the reverse order. The mind boggles at the thought of how many relationship break-ups or other domestic disasters were caused because our viewers took Russell's advice to "beware an apparently attractive offer," rather than to "grab all opportunities coming your way today". I shudder to think.

Shortly after the establishment of GSB, the government announced an opportunity to provide a new multi-channel service delivered through a conventional TV aerial, which looked set to rival the existing satellite and cable. It would initially carry fewer individual channel services, but would in theory be much easier and cheaper to install and run.

Always keen to colonise new opportunities, Granada came to an agreement for a joint venture with Carlton, which had won the franchise by displacing Thames Television in London. Carlton was run by Michael Green who was well known as being highly entrepreneurial but also highly mercurial and volatile. The two companies had also come to an agreement with Sky.

When the regulator insisted that Sky could not be part of the consortium, the two ITV companies should have backed away. Having Sky inside the tent was one thing, but having them outside was quite another. However a deal was done in which Sky would supply sport and other key programme services to the new platform, and work got under way to build it. There was much discussion about what the new service should be called, and eventually a highly-paid team of consultants came up with the name ONdigital.

"But I don't even know what that means," said Michael Green.

"If you're willing to spend £5 million on advertising," came the reply, "you can make it mean whatever you want it to mean." And they did.

The first CEO of ONdigital was a nice man called Stephen Grabiner who had been Marketing Director at The Daily Telegraph. Stephen put together a new team of younger people from cable and engineering backgrounds and set about building the service. As one of a very few people within Granada who knew anything at all about the fast-growing multi-channel world, I represented our company on the ONdigital board of directors. Others included Charles Allen and Steve Morrison from Granada, Michael Green and Nigel Walmsley from Carlton, also accompanied by a callow youth called David Cameron.

Michael Green was, as indicated, very enthusiastic and very excitable, but also very quick to temper and loud volumes. Whenever ONdigital board meetings were held in Carlton's headquarters next to Hyde Park Corner, you'd frequently hear the echoing sound of Michael screaming at some hapless executive at the top of his lungs. As often as not in my experience, the person cowering on the receiving end of these tirades was young Cameron.

The other person who frequently found himself on the wrong end of Michael's terrible temper was of course Stephen Grabiner himself, and it was only a question of time before the situation became untenable, the two of them fell out irretrievably, and Stephen was waiting at home for news of "what next". I'd become close to Stephen and had tried to be as supportive as I could, so that when I received a message over the weekend that Charles Allen and Michael Green wanted to see me first thing on the Monday morning, I assumed they wanted me to intervene with him to help make the peace. Instead the two of them sat me down and instantly let me know that the relationship with Stephen was beyond repair, and would I consider taking over as CEO of ONdigital? When I recovered my wits sufficiently to comprehend what they were telling me, I was able to answer succinctly.

"I'm very flattered that you've asked me, but I'm afraid that couldn't possibly work." Naturally they asked me why not. I was keen not to have to talk about my experience of growing up in the middle of two arguing adults, so I merely summarised. "Because I have personally witnessed the way that you, Michael, deal with people who work for you, and I know myself well enough to know that I wouldn't be able to tolerate that, even if I wanted to."

Charles Allen asked me to go into another room and to write on a piece of paper the conditions I would require if I were to accept the new job. I did, and my half a dozen rules included that I wasn't going to be yelled at, and that neither Michael nor Charles would be able to deal directly with anyone working for me. They should communicate with me, and I would deal with my staff.

It was Granada's Steve Morrison who once gave me some very helpful career advice; "it'll all be fun, and if it can't be fun, it'll be interesting." A little of what followed in the next two years was fun and interesting, but I'd have to say that most of it was just interesting. Among our most serious problems was that the conditional access cards which ONdigital users had to buy were quickly pirated and freely sold for a few pounds on the black market in pubs and at sporting events. It was only much later that we received information that the organisation which had allegedly originated the pirate cards was an Israeli company of which Sky's parent company, News Corp, was a shareholder.

When I look back on those days, I'm amazed at my own naivety in not properly comprehending the extent to which Tony Blair's government was in thrall to Rupert Murdoch and his evil empire. It's my more mature opinion that at that time, Murdoch and his minions were more or less writing broadcasting policy on cross-media ownership, and what we've subsequently learned about the way some of his journalists conducted themselves makes my skin crawl. I should have understood some of this better, because the evidence was all around us. When we had a visit to ONdigital by the then Minister of State for Trade and Industry, Patricia Hewitt, I took her to one side and told her that I might soon be asking her department to conduct an enquiry into reports that people with a connection to Sky may have been in some way behind the wave of piracy which was threatening fatally to undermine the digital terrestrial platform we were trying to build. Honestly, she couldn't have got herself out of the building any faster if I had loudly passed wind in her presence. The idea that her department would in some way confront Murdoch? What on earth was I thinking?

I did have another opportunity to raise the matter when I was called to give evidence to the House of Commons Select Committee on Culture, Media and Sport, under the chairmanship of Gerald Kaufman. The occasion remains especially memorable for me because I learned of the invitation while taking a winter holiday in the Maldives. The committee had requested my presence on the day after I was due to return home to the UK, so I spent the last few hours of my holiday wearing my swimming shorts and snorkelling above this staggeringly spectacular reef on which every colour, shape, and size of tropical fish was noodling around in search of plankton. As each fish opened its mouth, what seemed like tiny speech bubbles rose to the surface where they popped pointlessly. Twenty-four hours later, jet-lagged and readjusting, I was wearing my business suit and sitting in front of a horse-shoe shaped table and staring at serried rows of what seemed like Spitting Image characters. I remember noting that their wet lips were moving, but had absolutely no idea what they were saying.

To be fair to Michael Green, he did more or less stick to the undertakings he gave me when I took the job. Sometimes he'd call me up at home on a Sunday afternoon to talk about whatever was on his mind, and I'd begin to hear the volume of his voice rising, and also begin to sense my own pulse quickening. I could feel the faint stirrings of my deeply felt instinct to flee or fight, at which point I'd say, "Michael? We're not doing this. Remember?" and gradually he would calm down.

As CEO of the company, I'd be required to report to meetings of shareholders, and if at that time someone had said that in ten years from now one of the people in this room will be the Prime Minister, you'd have got to the lady who brought in the tea before anyone would have guessed David Cameron. Actually, now I come to reflect on it, Bella made a very good cup of tea and probably would have made a better fist of running the country. Much later when Cameron was Leader of the Opposition and I was a TV producer, I called his office to see if he'd like to talk about some "first 100 days" type coverage. I didn't get a reply, and suspect that his opinion of me was about the same as mine was of him. Unlike him, however, I didn't go on to ruin the country.

I did manage to persuade ONdigital's shareholders to put the weight of the ITV brand fully behind the new venture, in the course of which I found myself elevated yet again, now to become CEO of ITV. The Network Director at the time was David Liddiment, who had been my contemporary and, some might have said rival, when we both worked at Granada. I think David might have had some reservations about having me as his nominal boss at the Network Centre, but fortunately he was and is probably the most talented TV executive I've ever met, so I was able to reassure him that my only intention would be to back him up. My time back at ITV was a welcome return to more mainstream television, and I played a small role in handling incidents such as the Who Wants to be a Millionaire "Coughing

Major". At one point I found myself standing on the stage in front of several hundred advertisers at the Odeon Leicester Square, presenting the latest ITV schedule alongside David Liddiment and Ant and Dec (lovely guys), and it was all a bit of a whirlwind.

However it's fair to say that this was an absolutely bloody awful time for ITV. The easing of media ownership restrictions meant that the original fifteen regional companies had now consolidated down to five – Scottish, Meridian (UNM), Central, Carlton and Granada – and these handful were locked in a winner-takes-all battle for who would emerge as the ultimate single owner. This meant that every decision we made at the Network Centre which benefitted one of them was likely to be opposed and resented by one or more of the others. The Finance Director of one company put it to me bluntly: "every time you give a commission that puts a million pounds on the profits of another company, it will cost me an extra ten million when I come to buy them." So while our core remit was to commission the programmes which would most strongly benefit the overall ITV schedule, now we were at the same time under pressure to take account of inter-company politics. Equally, the need in each company to increase their bottom-lines, and therefore to increase their value when it came time to sell, meant that production budgets, and consequently programme quality, were suffering. As former producers ourselves, David and I still had strong links directly back into the programme-making community, so we received direct information about the deep budget cuts our former colleagues were being required to make. ITV had come a long way from David Plowright's mantra that "everyone who isn't a programme-maker, works for the programme-makers." The situation led to nasty confrontations and some loud and bad- tempered rows between those who cared most about the programmes and those who cared most about the profits. All very interesting, but certainly not fun.

On the lighter side, David and I were among the ITV executives assigned to greet Her Majesty the Queen that year at the Royal

Command Performance. I'd been up close on a few occasions during my time as a reporter and producer, but this would be the first occasion on which I'd actually be introduced. We were a bit nervous as she entered the theatre and we all stood in line to shake hands, and she was radiant and absolutely delightful.

The programme that year was to include a performance from the cast of the hit musical The Full Monty, and the producers thought it would be good fun for the "miners" to do their famous routine in which they strip off their clothes. Obviously there was a delicate question of decorum and decency, and the idea was that when they got down to removing their last garments, they would stand for just the tiniest fraction of a second before the lights plunged the auditorium into darkness, thereby sparing any blushes. The Full Monty dancers would be the last act before the interval.

It was all going well, the act was good fun and the clothes were coming off with suitable abandon. The row of fit young men got down to their last items of clothing, ripped them off, and turned to face the audience. One one thousand, two one thousand, three one thousand … the line of stark naked men remained in full view for what must have been five seconds, before the lights went down and everyone retired for the intermission. Nothing was said, and the remainder of the performance went as planned.

On the following evening, as was traditional, Her Majesty hosted a reception for the performers and producers at Buckingham Palace. It was all very convivial, some drink was taken, and at one point David and I found ourselves in conversation with the Queen.

"I do apologise," said David, "if the act by The Full Monty caused any distress or embarrassment to Your Majesty."

The Queen responded with a cheeky grin, raised her glass and said in a girlish voice, "Oh, I didn't mind a bit," and then tottered off to get a refill.

BACK TO BASICS

———

When ITV Digital's shareholders, Carlton and Granada, walked away from a £315m commitment to buy the rights to the Football League, the new platform went bust and the City and markets wanted a scapegoat. At the same time the remaining ITV companies were in the final stages of consolidation, and I could see a couple of years ahead during which I'd be required to sack all my friends, at the end of which they'd almost certainly sack me. So I told my board that if they needed a head, I'd willingly go to the guillotine. Which I did.

Some of those close to events obviously felt it would have been more appropriate for one or more of the shareholders to take the wrap, and Greg Dyke was memorably quoted coining the phrase that "deputy-heads will roll." I found myself on the receiving end of a minor but very welcome wave of support and sympathy from a few nice people in the industry, but truth to tell, I simply couldn't wait to get back to what I'd joined TV to do in the first place, which was to produce programmes.

So on the Friday I said goodbye to my loyal and long-suffering PA Marian Woods, and also to my luxury company car, use of a driver, a very high salary and index-linked pension. By the Monday I had packed away my suits, ties and smart shoes, had reinvented myself as an independent producer and was being kept waiting for twenty-five minutes in the front hallway of Channel 5 to see the commissioning editor for factual programmes. You could say that I needed a sense of humour, and luckily I had one.

I first of all collaborated with my wonderful and highly respected friend Andrea Wonfor, who had recently left an important job at Channel 4 and was keen to set up as an indie. Andrea had a well-deserved reputation as a one-woman powerhouse of TV production – having been responsible for the iconic music series The Tube, discovering and featuring Jools Holland and Paula Yates in the process, and thereby putting Tyne Tees Television on the national map in an unprecedented fashion. Andrea lived and wanted to stay based in Newcastle while I would remain in London. We called our company Liberty Bell, which struck a chord of newly found freedom with me because returning to programme-making already felt like putting down two heavy suitcases. I borrowed temporary offices from my friend William Burdett-Coutts who ran the Riverside Studios in Hammersmith and made my bicycle my default means of transport to and from work, and to and from what quickly turned into dozens of meetings with commissioning editors from all the channels.

Sadly Andrea was diagnosed with breast cancer within a very few weeks and withdrew from the company so that she could concentrate on battling her illness. She did so with her customary courage and dignity, but tragically she died within a few months. Andrea was a wonderful and inspirational woman who is sorely missed by friends and family and colleagues.

Working with William at the Riverside Studios was an old mate and colleague from Granada days called David Buckley, and Dave quickly offered to help me to get started. As part of my severance deal with ITV, it had been agreed that they'd commission me to make a few documentaries, and the first one was on the subject of so-called white-collar boxing, in which businessmen and executives show off how alpha male they are by taking to the ring. I was introduced to a very talented director called Southan Morris who came on board to help Dave and I to make the show.

Having been known within the industry for the previous few years as "a suit", it was important for me to find ways to remind people that I had originally been a pretty good producer. I think I must have benefitted from a mix of sympathy and curiosity in the wider industry, because the then head of BBC2 Jane Root, agreed to have breakfast with me so that I could pick her sizeable brain about starting up and running an independent production company.

She gave me the same good advice that is often given by publishers to authors, which is some variation of "write about what you know." By chance I had just read a newspaper report of a survey which found that the 35–54 age group of men was the grumpiest in history; grumpier than their parents who had survived the war and were grateful for having done so; grumpier than their children who were preoccupied with their careers and had expectations of becoming home-owners. This was the group who were least likely to say that our political leaders know better than us, that things were generally getting better, and were irritated by just about every aspect of modern life. It was the generation who'd grown up in an era of flower power and free love, and who felt they'd been promised a bright shining future in which robots did the hard graft. Instead those of us who were working were working harder than ever, and mobile phones meant the end of sneaking off and making yourself uncontactable for a happy hour or so.

At that moment I was 51, and I definitely recognised the phenomenon. So I pitched to Jane an idea called Grumpy Old Men, in which a collection of 35-54 year olds would generally gripe about what men like me found irritating. Everything from mobile phones to bad grammar, from multi-storey carparks to body-piercing, from idiotic slogans like "Fanatical about Film" to not knowing whether we were still allowed to open doors for women or give up our seats on public transport. The list was, happily for me, endless.

To her lasting credit, and to my lasting delight, Jane got the idea immediately. "I'm sometimes married to one," she said.

"Does that mean the man you are married to is sometimes grumpy?" I asked, "or that you are sometimes married to a grumpy old man and sometimes to someone else?" Pedantry was an important aspect of being one.

Jane passed my programme pitch to Jo Clinton-Davis who looked after popular factual for the BBC. Jo also liked the idea but, no doubt wondering if it could sustain through a series, asked me for more detail of the things that irritated grumpy old men. Two days later I sent her fifteen pages which, she later told me, gave her the best laugh she'd had for ages. I was off to the races. I was introduced to another like-minded producer who was instantly recognisable as a grumpy called Alan Lewens. Alan helped me to recruit a cast of clever and funny men which included Rick Wakeman, Bob Geldof, Arthur Smith, Rory McGrath, Tim Rice, Don Warrington, Richard Madeley, Nigel Havers, Tony Hawks, John Sessions, Felix Dexter, Bill Nighy, Will Self, John O'Farrell, and Tony Slattery.

We'd sit them down for an interview, and simply say stuff like "designer labels" or "bottled water" and off they'd go, ranting on about whatever aspect of the thing got on their nerves. In the editing room we intercut short comments together with relevant archive footage, and the result was a riot. The final addition of the unique and lugubrious voice of the brilliant actor Geoffrey Palmer made our original script at least twenty per cent funnier. What a lovely man he was.

When I heard that BBC2 had put clips from our series at the top of their seasonal showreel, and that the invited audience of hard-bitten reviewers had been laughing out loud, I knew we were on to something. Then, on the morning after the first episode was transmitted, I was in the queue at the post office when I overheard a conversation between the postmaster and a customer.

"Did you see that programme about grumpy old men last night?"

"We did, and my husband and I agreed with every single word they said!"

"So did we! We laughed our heads off, and my wife said she was expecting me to pop up at any second."

They went on to chat about some of the stuff in the show, but for this one time I wasn't being made to feel grumpy about being kept waiting in the queue while the people ahead of me behaved as though I was invisible. At that moment I'd worked as a news reporter for the BBC for five years, then as a current affairs producer and editor in ITV for another twenty, and this was the first time I'd ever heard members of the viewing audience having a casual conversation about one of my programmes.

We made three series of Grumpy Old Men, then several more of Grumpy Old Women, then Grumpy Old Christmas, Grumpy Old Holidays and Grumpy Old New Year. In the end the Grumpy phenomenon became a total of seventy-three programmes, five books written by me and several more by my friend and colleague Judith Holder, and a touring stage show. Give yourself a treat and watch a few of the programmes on YouTube.

Our success in producing the grumpies enabled us to win a commission to make a new version of Three Men in a Boat, this time featuring Griff Rhys-Jones, Rory McGrath, and the then young and emerging Dara O'Briain. All three were very smart and genuinely funny, and the show was recommissioned for three more series.

Running my own company was joyful from the very start. Suddenly, for the first time in years, I wasn't obliged to go to endless meetings with boring people talking about marketing, ratings and advertising revenue. I could control my own priorities and my own diary. Right from the start, Dave and I instituted what we called our "no arseholes" rule, which meant that you might sometimes have to work for someone you didn't much like, but you'd never have to sit next to them. We'd hire only nice people who cared more about what we put on the screen than what we put in our pockets. We did well and we had fun: Dave and I used to say that the worst day in Liberty Bell was better than the best day in ITV, and it was.

My experience of commissioning so many factual programmes for ITV gave me the benefit of knowing some of what the channels were looking for, and of course all that time working with talented producers and presenters now proved to be advantageous. Among the remarkable people I'd met was the writer and singer Marsha Hunt. Marsha was probably best known, at the time, because her fabulously extravagant Afro had provided the emblematic silhouette promoting the rock musical "Hair". She had also performed at the Isle of Wight festival on the same bill as Jimi Hendrix, where she'd worn the first pair of hot pants any of us had seen, and which shortly thereafter became ubiquitous. Marsha was also known as a former girlfriend of Mick Jagger, with whom she had a daughter, Karis. She was a talented writer of fiction and non-fiction, and I'd commissioned an Irish producer called Alan Gilsenan to make an episode of a series called "God Bless America" in which writers gave us a guided tour through the cities in which they'd situated their books. Gore Vidal's Washington was one, Scott Turow did Chicago, and Marsha had taken us around her life and times in Philadelphia.

Marsha had become a friend, so I was shocked and saddened when she called me one day to say that she had been diagnosed with breast cancer. She wasn't afraid, but had been told that she needed to undergo a single mastectomy operation, which was going ahead in two days' time. Did we want to make a documentary about her experience? Obviously this didn't give us enough notice to find a broadcaster, but we sent a crew to her home in Ireland anyway and began recording.

You can probably guess that Marsha was incredibly brave and inspirational, and anyone who knows her won't be surprised that she instantly rejected the suggestion that she should have reconstructive surgery to disguise her missing breast. "I consider it a war wound from my battle," she said, "and I'm proud to have emerged victorious." When asked if she was concerned that men might find her less attractive, she'd let out an uproarious and infectious cackle which all her friends would instantly recognise. "If any man would find me less interesting because of something like that, he's not someone I'd want to know anyway."

Marsha introduced me to her friend, the society photographer (Lord) Patrick Lichfield, who, some years earlier had taken what at the time was considered to be a very risqué studio photograph of Marsha sitting on the floor, completely naked. Our idea for the film was that Patrick would take the same photograph again, some three decades later, showing Marsha looking every bit as striking and beautiful, notwithstanding the radical surgery. He did, and the two images set alongside each other told her story. She was the same strong and proud woman, but now she was also a cancer survivor.

Patrick was open and entertaining and a fount of great anecdotes about his life and work. He was famous for his portraits of members of the Royal family, but also for his studies of some of the world's most beautiful women, photographed in discreet but erotic poses and settings; exactly the sort of thing which would be widely disapproved of today. I remember him telling me that every famous supermodel he had ever photographed harboured some personal phobia about an aspect of their appearance. "Surely you can see that my nose is too big?" or "Patrick, please could you try to disguise my fat thighs?"

One of Patrick's best stories involved his friendship with Princess Margaret who was also a neighbour of his on the glamorous Caribbean island of Mustique. What Margaret and other famous people liked about the private island was that it didn't matter who you were, no-one took particular notice, and everyone was treated the same. No special fuss was made for rock stars, movie stars, celebrity photographers or Royalty.

To illustrate the point, I'll retell Patrick's story in what I can remember of his own words.

"I was holidaying on the island when one evening I took a call from Margaret who asked if I'd like to join a group of friends for dinner at Basil's bar. When I arrived, I discovered that Margaret was there with Roddy Llewellyn, and the other guests were Mick and Bianca Jagger, and Raquel Welch. The six of us had a long and delightful evening during which lots of food was eaten and a great deal of alcohol was drunk. I was having a lovely time, but after quite a few hours, I saw that Margaret was indicating to me that I ought to go to the bar to sign the bill.

"I wasn't especially keen to do so because this bill was going to be a very big one, but nonetheless I got to my feet and started walking towards the bar. At the same time I noticed that Raquel Welch was also standing and heading in the same direction, and so I slowed down, perfectly happy that she should get there before me. As it happened, I arrived alongside her just as she was scribbling her name, and she turned the paper around to hand it to the waiter. He examined it carefully, and appeared to be struggling to decipher the second part of what she'd written. "Welch," she said helpfully, and then said it again. Still frowning, the waiter returned it to her. 'I'm very sorry,' he said, 'we need your surname, not your nationality'."

Following her surgery, Marsha was prescribed a course of chemotherapy from which she seemed certain to lose her magnificent hair. Instead of waiting to see what would transpire, she organised a family party at which her grandchildren were invited to have fun cutting it all off and then watching while she shaved her head – laughing all the while. Of course she looked every bit as fabulous completely bald as she had with her Afro. The resulting personal diary of Marsha's journey through her illness is inspirational, and latterly gave hope to many women who found themselves in a similar situation. Today Marsha lives in France, and is every bit as crazy and marvellous as ever she was.

One day I took a call from Chris Shaw who was the commissioning editor for factual programmes at Channel 5. I'd known Chris a bit from his days at ITN, and he was calling to tell me that in the time since Tony Blair's spin doctor Alastair Campbell had left his job in Downing Street, all the channels had been chasing him with a view to making some programmes. Channel 5 had won the battle and now they needed a producer to make them. Would I like to do it? Needless to say I was absolutely delighted. "Why me?" I asked. "Because he's a very strong character and we might need someone who is able to say no to him." I took that as a compliment, and was very excited indeed by the opportunity.

The package of programmes agreed with Alastair included a documentary following him in the weeks after his resignation, and a series of interviews with some high-profile people he admired. The first of these would be an opportunity to get inside Alastair's head just a bit, and to tell some of his life-story. The second would allow access and insight into some prominent people who wouldn't normally sit down for a one-to-one. I was able to hire a very clever, very experienced, very impressive producer/director called Judith Dawson who had formerly been a political editor for Sky News. Judith already had a relationship based on mutual respect with Alastair. I also enjoyed meeting Alastair's partner Fiona, who is a smart, highly principled and (as Alastair would be the first to admit) long-suffering woman.

Alastair is of course a larger-than-life character and we got along well from the start. He and I are about the same height and weight, though of course he is younger and fitter than I am. We're also both a bit crazy, though he is also far madder than me. Anyone who knows Alastair knows that the main thing about him is that whatever he does, he does to excess. In his earlier life as a newspaper journalist, and like many people on Fleet Street in those days, he drank a lot of alcohol. Far too much. In those days, and latter days working for Tony Blair, he was undoubtedly a workaholic. They never stopped. At the time I met him he'd just been through one of the most god-awful experiences it's possible to imagine in public life. The row with the

BBC over its report by Andrew Gilligan, followed by the death of David Kelly would take its toll on anyone. Alastair had been right in the eye of the storm, and this was the first time in years that he was allowing himself to get his life back.

Some people in such a situation would very sensibly decide it would be a good idea to regain some fitness, but obviously that wasn't going to be enough for Alastair; he was going to do a triathlon – running, cycling and swimming. He duly set about the training like a man possessed, and it didn't need a shrink to work out what was going on.

At the same time, Alastair was leafing through his contacts book to work out who to interview for the agreed series of Channel 5 programmes, and among his first choices was the champion cyclist Lance Armstrong. At this point Lance had won the Tour de France cycle race seven times, which many people believed would have been impossible without the use of performance enhancing drugs, but Lance was consistently denying it and Alastair was inclined to believe him. The fact that Lance had also bounced back in an extraordinary and even superhuman way from testicular cancer made him all the more appealing for Alastair; that he had achieved what he had in the face of all that adversity made him even more impressive.

Judith and I duly read up all the background on the history of drug-taking in cycling and the measures taken by the sport to combat it, immersing ourselves in a quest to understand just exactly how extraordinary were Lance's achievements. Alastair argued that so rigorous was the testing regime that it would be impossible for someone like Lance to get away with it. He had been tested and tested and tested, and if there was something to find, the authorities would have found it. Judith and I came to the view that one way or another he must have cheated, but Alastair was inclined to give the benefit of the doubt.

Lance had agreed to the interview and we all dutifully schlepped to France where he was due to be training. I have a feeling that the experience for Alastair was a bit like it was for me after I stopped being the CEO of ITV and next day was a humble producer. For a long time working for Tony Blair, Alastair had been used to a private plane waiting on the tarmac for whenever the passengers were ready, and then getting priority over airspace to wherever you were landing. I think that on this occasion we travelled on Easyjet. I probably don't need to add anything. It's fair to say that he took it all in good part and retained his sense of humour throughout.

We eventually arrived at a settlement of luxury Winnebagos which were serving as Lance's training camp, and sent in word that we'd arrived and were setting up for the interview. We were aware that Lance was just inside one of the caravans, and was eating lunch with his then girlfriend, the rock musician Sheryl Crow. He didn't come out or acknowledge us in any way, and we sat patiently for about forty minutes until he was good and ready.

Eventually he emerged to meet us, was friendly but formal with Alastair, more or less ignored the rest of us, and eventually sat down to do the interview. Lance had obviously been asked the same questions dozens of times and was ready with his stock answers, but still Alastair let him off the allegations of drug-use too easily for my taste. Anyway we got the interview, and when it was over we asked if we could do some setting up shots of him walking and talking with Alastair, which he refused. We asked if we could shoot some footage of him doing some training or chatting with team-mates, or preparing in any way, and he refused. He had done the minimum he'd said he was going to do and that was that. I'd arrived feeling sceptical about Lance Armstrong, and left with the strong view that he was an arrogant arse. The resulting programme was okay but unremarkable. I think Alastair was genuinely disappointed when it eventually emerged that Lance had been doping and lying comprehensively for many years.

Later we recorded an interview between Alastair and Peter Mandelson, with whom he'd had a long and close but up and down relationship. For students of politics such as Judith and I, this was an absolutely delicious treat. The two of them went over their individual memories of the birth of New Labour, then through their various crises, and eventually came to talk about Peter's second resignation from the Cabinet. "Well you'd know more about that than I would," said Peter, at which point Alastair went on to accept that maybe he'd got it wrong and had been in part responsible for Mandelson being forced to go. A little bit of political history.

Most exciting of all was the news that former US President Bill Clinton was coming to town to promote his memoirs and Alastair would get the only long-form interview he was going to grant. I'd previously managed to grab a quick word with Jimmy Carter when he'd visited Newcastle when I was a young reporter, so this would be my second American president.

The subject of charisma is always interesting; it's a quality that's much easier to spot than to define, and over the years I've been lucky to meet a lot of people blessed with it. When trying to understand the ingredients, it's difficult to separate what you know about someone in advance from your actual experience of them in the flesh. In the case of Bill Clinton, the fact that a posse of armed secret service agents arrive several hours ahead of him and start scouring the place may be a factor. However it doesn't explain why every woman in the office was absolutely desperate to find a reason to join us on the shoot. I've never dealt with anyone who created such excitement in everyone within half a mile of the project.

The former President was scheduled to give the interview while passing through the Ritz Hotel in Piccadilly, and Southan, Judith and I arrived several hours in advance to ensure that everything would go without a hitch. We were shown into a highly ornate suite on the roadside of the hotel, but Southan and the cameraman John Sorapure were keen not to use the neoclassical surroundings as the backdrop, preferring the large window and the view of the trees outside. This can sometimes cause technical problems as the outside light changes with the passing clouds, so John painstakingly attached a thin layer of tinted plastic sheeting to the window frame, making sure that it couldn't be seen on camera. It's a subtle technique but an effective way of giving the cameraman control of the natural light outside.

Did we imagine the frisson of excitement which seemed to vibrate through the building as the great man and his entourage approached, or was it in some way tangible? I wonder what it must be like to be this bloke. At the centre of a constantly moving organism, the proboscis of it operating ahead of you, the rear of it following up behind you, and a whole entity surrounding you on all sides with no purpose other than to service you and your needs. That's how important you are. No wonder they so seldom manage to keep their feet on the ground.

After what seems to be endless expectation and suspense, at last Bill Clinton walks through the door, and of course at this point in what is undoubtedly a whistle-stop tour, he's probably relieved to be meeting someone he knows. He and Alastair and Tony have been through a lot together over the years, and no doubt it's right to describe them as old friends. They greet each other warmly and are relaxed. The rest of us are not.

Usually when you meet people you've only ever seen on the telly, they turn out to be smaller than you think they're going to be. In this case, Bill Clinton was bigger than I thought he was going to be. Alastair introduced him to Judith, then to me, and we shook hands. In my four decades in television up to that point, I've never asked anyone if I could have a photograph taken with them, but this was the closest I've come. These were the days "pre-selfies".

Even despite the warmth of the relationship, the President was on a tight timetable and so we were not going to be given any more than the allocated time. So you might be able to imagine how I felt when, fifteen minutes after we'd started the interview, the tape holding the tinted plastic sheets over the windows came unstuck and suddenly the room was flooded with direct sunlight. Everyone looked at each other, dismayed.

"Let's just do it with natural light," I said. Not a possibility, apparently. Anything we now shot in natural light wouldn't match the footage we'd shot already. Agonising seconds and then minutes passed while the cameraman climbed up on a desk, and then on a ladder, trying to re-attach the plastic. I could see that Alastair was getting irritated. Clinton was not irritated but was definitely going to leave at the appointed time. I was hyperventilating. How, the fucking fuck, could this be happening? Were three hours not quite enough time to prepare properly? It doesn't happen very often, especially not in a work context, but I was bloody furious.

Eventually of course the problem was solved, we ran the cameras, Alastair conducted a very professional interview during which nothing was said that hadn't been said many times before, but we'd got it in the can. It was a good day and another remarkable and exhilarating experience.

Alastair went on to edit and publish vast extracts from a detailed diary he kept for the entire time that he worked with Tony Blair, which Judith and I enjoyed turning into several fascinating programmes for BBC2. The rest is … the rest.

All this while we had been further developing our "grumpy old …" franchise, but by now Jane Root had left BBC2 and her place as Controller had been taken over by Roly Keating. Roly had previously been in charge of the BBC's arts and music and was obviously an estimable character, but I had no idea whether he had much of a sense of humour. When he asked to meet me to discuss the possibility of a new series of Grumpy Old Men, I knew that the challenge would be to persuade him that there was an ongoing stream of irritations which continued to make grumpy old men grumpy. So I armed myself with long list, and to illustrate the point, I popped into a pharmacy on my way to the meeting and purchased a new toothbrush, which I handed to Roly, still in its packaging.

"While we're chatting," I said, "just see if you can get into that." He got the joke, had a brief but futile attempt to penetrate the clear plastic wrapping, and then put it down while we talked. "No no," I said, "you've given up far too easily." I think maybe he commissioned a new series just to get me out of his office. Roly is a delightful bloke, who went on to take over the British Library and was recently knighted.

Meanwhile my Newcastle-based colleague Judith Holder had taken hold of Grumpy Old Women and was extending it at least as far as the original. Judith had a natural feel for the female equivalents of the kinds of things which irritated men, and had assembled a cast of very funny and smart women which included Jenny Éclair, Linda Robson, Germaine Greer, Kathryn Flett, Arabella Weir, Sheila Hancock, Janet Street-Porter and Jilly Cooper. Judith's funny commentary script was read by the marvellous Alison Steadman.

The continuing success of the franchise, as well as the other shows we were producing alongside it, meant that Liberty Bell had become quite a successful but still small independent company in a short time. Maybe I was three or four years in when I was approached by Jon Thoday, who is one of the bosses at Avalon, to ask if I'd be interested in cooperating to produce a stage show based on Grumpy Old Men. I'm usually up for new ideas and challenges so I was attracted to the idea, but my main concern was that the authentic grumpy old men were probably genuinely too actually grumpy to commit to the work and discipline necessary. But maybe the women might do so?

In the same conversation, Jon asked me what it would take to persuade me to sell the company. Keeping in mind that anyone buying a TV production company would normally require the existing management to stay on for a few years to run it, I said, "I'd sell it to anyone who'd give me the amount of money I want and who'd promise to leave me alone." "I'll do that," said Jon, and he did. The only thing he insisted on was that we should move our offices a couple of miles up the road into some space in the existing Avalon building in Notting Hill. That was a nuisance but not a deal-breaker. Other than that, little changed, and we continued as a thriving company but now under the Avalon umbrella.

The deal gave me a welcome level of financial security, as a result of which I exchanged my family home in Kingston for a smaller apartment next to the river, and bought a derelict but potentially lovely house in the New Forest. I'd work long hours for four days a week in town, and then spend a three-day weekend in the country. I've owned and run a motorcycle consistently since the age of sixteen, and so my commute back and forth to Notting Hill was tolerable. It was a horrible experience when my shiny blue BMW 1200 was stolen from outside the Avalon offices one afternoon, but plenty of worse things happen.

In most of the shows made by Liberty Bell I played the role of executive producer. What's that exactly? I always say that the executive producer does as little as possible but as much as necessary. What that means is that the producer or the director or the producer/director does most of the hands-on hard work, while the exec producer steers the ship. However that's not nothing; it usually means having the idea, pitching it to the commissioning broadcaster, developing it further to a point where it's a commission, casting the key editorial people, and eventually viewing and commenting on a rough edit of the show so it gets to the point of delivery to the broadcaster. The joy of the role of executive producer is seeing your ideas come to fruition and working with some very talented and very affable creative people. The frustration is that sometimes you feel further away from the real creativity than you necessarily want to be.

I solved this at the time by hands-on producing a few programmes myself, one of which was a single documentary for BBC2 in which a group of recently bereaved women talked about the experience of losing their husbands. It sounds very maudlin, but actually turned into an opportunity for them to celebrate their lives with their spouses, and to share experiences of dealing with an event which is rarely spoken about openly. The programme was called "The Widow's Tale," and the cast included the brilliant Jayne Zito, whose husband had been stabbed by a paranoid schizophrenic while waiting on the platform of the London underground. Jayne went on to establish a charity to benefit exactly the kind of disturbed person who had committed the murder. Also the well-known agony aunt Katherine Whitehorn, who spoke movingly about the loss of her husband, the spy-thriller writer Gavin Lyall. Katherine had written that "You don't 'get over' the man, though you do after a year or two get over the death. But you have to learn to live in another country in which you're an unwilling refugee." Just by way of contrast, I interviewed Joan Rivers, whose husband had taken his own life, thereby devastating their daughter and herself. Between laughing and crying, Joan told us that "when I get to heaven, if I find him there, I'm going to kill him all over again for what he did to us."

Another of the single films I produced at the time was memorably called "What I Wish I'd Known When I Was 20". It was another single one-hour for BBC2, and everything about this show was delightful, including the self-explanatory title. The idea was to take a group of interesting people from different walks of life, all of whom were over the age of sixty, and ask them the question. We broke down the subject into separate sections such as "what I wish I'd known when I was 20 about … relationships, work/life balance, bringing up children, drink and drugs, money," etc. We got the chance to assemble an absolutely magnificent cast which included the barrister and playwright John Mortimer, the fashion designer Mary Quant, the jazz musician George Melly, the American comedienne Joan Rivers, the photographer Patrick Lichfield, and my friend Joan Bakewell. I interviewed them all separately, asking more or less exactly the same questions, and we edited their answers together in a sort of vox-pop, illustrated by old photos or archive home movie of each of them growing up.

The format gave them the chance to reflect at leisure on aspects of their interesting lives and, although I don't think it revealed much in the way of earth-shattering insights, it provided a fascinating perspective on the the times they'd lived through. At the end of the show I asked each of them, "if you could give your twenty year old self one piece of advice, what would it be?" Answers ranged from "don't sweat the small stuff," through "follow your passions," to "try to be happy." My favourite, however, was from Joan Bakewell who paused for a moment and then said, "get as much sex as you can."

STORYVAULT

I had sold Liberty Bell to the Avalon Group of companies, but was still in the middle of an agreed three year earn-out, when I was contacted one day by someone called Sam Richards who said she had been advised to see me by Elaine Bedell, who was a commissioning editor at the BBC. Elaine was interested in an idea Sam had for a factual series featuring the clinical psychologist Tanya Byron and they needed a producer to make it happen. Could she come in for a chat?

It was rare but always nice when new and interesting projects fell into our lap, and I was happy to take the meeting. Sam had previously worked as a theatrical agent in Los Angeles and London, and was highly respected and well-connected on her side of the industry. Her idea was a good one, but she had no experience as a producer. Sam came across as smart, open and easy to deal with, so we agreed to develop a four-part series which was to be called Am I Normal?

I asked my former colleague from World in Action Eamon O'Connor to produce, and Sam stayed alongside, partly to learn more about the business and partly to look after Tanya, who was her friend and client. There's no reason to go into details or to apportion blame, but not to put too fine a point on it, the production had more than its share of difficulties. The series eventually went out on BBC2, and while none of it had been Sam's fault and we hadn't actually fallen out, at that time my expectation was that we were unlikely to work together in the future.

However from the start Sam was full of good ideas, and one day she came to me with a short piece of video which she asked me to look at. It was a brief clip showing a man called Willie Harcourt-Cooze, who was the husband of her friend Tania Harcourt-Cooze, better known as the stylish model Tania Coleridge. Willie and Tania had discovered and bought a cacao farm deep in a backwater of Venezuela, and had a dream to bring the beans to England where they would set up a business producing the finest chocolate in the world. In the clip he seemed like a sort of modern-day Tarzan, swinging through the trees, handsome and charismatic.

"And this guy has never been on the telly?" I asked.

He hadn't, and so we set about finding someone who would give us some money to develop and pitch the idea as a series. It was eventually commissioned by Walter Iuzzolino at Channel 4, and directed by our good friend Southan Morris. We called it Willie's Wonky Chocolate Factory and Willie became a minor star. With the help of the TV exposure, his chocolate found its way into Selfridges, Waitrose and many other places, where it can still be found to this day. The idea turned into two series and a Christmas special.

By now I had completed the three years that I'd undertaken to remain with Liberty Bell under its new ownership, and indeed had worked for an additional eighteen months longer than my contractual obligation, but now instead of having my own company, once again I was effectively employed by someone else. I was still enjoying the actual work, so when Southan Morris and Sam Richards asked me if I'd like to start a new indie with them, I was tempted. Southan is simply the best director I've ever worked with; the spark of genius that he'd added to so many of our Liberty Bell shows was a big part of the reason for our success. In addition to being exceptionally well connected with talent, Sam had loads of ideas for new programmes which would enable us to expand the repertoire of possible new commissions. So the idea of cooperating in a new venture with the pair of them had many attractions. However Avalon had always been fair to me and so I told Southan and Sam that I'd only cooperate in a new company if we could form it under the Avalon banner. They agreed, but when I tried to convince Avalon of the appeal of the idea, they didn't want to know.

After trying my best to persuade them, I eventually told the bosses at Avalon that if they didn't want to start the new company, I'd probably leave and do so anyway. They remained unconvinced, which is how Storyvault Films began. It started as an equal partnership between Sam, Southan, my long-time friend and colleague David Buckley and myself.

We chose to call the new business Storyvault Films because it corresponded with the name of a website which I was in the process of launching in partnership with my friend Simon Dore. I'd had the idea shortly after my father died, at aged 75. I've mentioned before that Dad had been orphaned at fourteen, had fended for himself until he was old enough to join the army, had fought in World War 2, was sent as part of the force policing the United Nations Mandate in Palestine, got married, had two sons, and worked for an insurance company for twenty-five years, and that's just about everything I know about him. He had been the last of his generation in our family, and now it was too late to ask him the many questions which would have filled in the gaps. I had no excuses because I've been a TV producer all my life, but then I realised that none of us has any excuse because, for the first time in human history, just about all of us are walking around with a high-quality digital camera in our pockets.

So the idea behind the Storyvault.com website is to encourage people to record interviews with their parents, grandparents, neighbours or family friends, and to upload them onto the platform. The videos then become a treasured archive for the next generation of the

207

family, but also are searchable by students of history wishing to access first hand witness accounts of events from living memory. Someone doing a project about the Windrush can go on the site and find the vivid recollections of people who came to Britain in the fifties and sixties, and anyone researching the fall of the Berlin Wall can access and watch interviews with people who were there. Storyvault – a safe place to keep your stories. Storyvault.com. Have a look. Interview your loved ones. It's important.

Now the four of us; Dave, Southan, Sam and I were desperately thinking up ideas for new programmes to pitch to broadcasters. In our efforts to broaden our appeal and repertoire, we were fortunate to meet and bring into the company the distinguished and much-respected documentary maker Olivia Lichtenstein, who joined us as a shareholder/director. So now we were five.

One of our outstanding past productions had been our coverage of the so-called Fourth Plinth project which was organised by Antony Gormley in Trafalgar Square. The sculptor had invited applications from anyone who wanted to occupy the empty plinth outside the National Gallery for a period of forty-five minutes. There'd be a fifteen-minute changeover, and then the next person would take their place and do their thing. There were actors, musicians, dancers, models, performance art and every kind of fun stuff.

We set up an outside broadcast unit in the Square and broadcast the process live on the Sky Arts channel, and then also edited and packaged some highlight programmes. Sky Arts at that time was a very marginal digital service available only to customers who bought a rather expensive package of pay channels, and therefore the on-air audience was small. So small, in fact, that I strongly suspected that far more people saw and noted the coverage by walking past it than by seeing it on the TV.

The whole project was good fun, and I watched carefully as passers-by seemed to notice the event, register the "Sky Arts" signage, and then remark that they'd thought that Sky was all about sport and movies; who knew they also had a channel dedicated to Arts? That seemed to be a key ingredient in what Sky regarded as a success.

When we were considering new ideas for programmes to pitch to Sky, we took into account that ideally it should take place in public, that the TV coverage should in some way enhance the original art, and would leave a legacy so that Sky Arts' contribution to the culture of the nation would remain in evidence. Between us we came up with the idea of a competition for artists in which the prize would be a £10,000 commission for an artwork which would then be displayed in a national gallery. Our first thought was Portrait Artist of the Year, the second was Landscape Artist of the Year, and we pitched both to Sky.

Shows about art are notoriously difficult to bring audiences to, mostly because there's a widespread belief that somehow you have to be a very clever person to "get it". I told Sky that the Portraits show would be popular and feel accessible for the very same reason that there's usually a queue outside Madame Tussauds; no one is afraid to look at a portrait and say, "it doesn't even look like the sitter!" When the viewers disagreed with the judges, it would be "shout at the telly," telly. There was lots of scepticism and resistance among some members of the commissioning team – one of them memorably asking us if we were really going to be asking viewers to sit and watch paint dry - but with steadfast help and support from Phil Edgar-Jones, Mark Sammon and James Hunt, we got the go-ahead for the first series.

The commission enabled us to hire a new Series Editor, and we were lucky to find Danielle Graham who'd previously worked on The Culture Show and The Apprentice. Dan quickly turned out to be another brilliant colleague, full of energy and ideas, who would eventually join us as the sixth shareholder/director of the company.

Our first challenge was to cast the presenters, and we immediately knew that we'd want two people, one who would give the show credibility among the Arts establishment, and the other whose presence would indicate that this was a show for a general audience; that you didn't have to be an expert to be able to appreciate and enjoy it.

Ever since I first got to know Joan Bakewell when we both worked at Granada in the late 1980s, I've grabbed every chance I was ever given to work with her. Leaving aside the fact that she's always been strikingly beautiful, she is also very clever, good fun and her default answer to any question was usually "yes". Her reputation and credibility in the cultural community was second to none.

"But Joan is eighty years old!" said one or two of our colleagues.

"Yes she is," I answered, "and it's my greatest wish to still be employing her when she's ninety."

Danielle suggested casting Frank Skinner as the other presenter because while he is funny and quick-witted, he doesn't come across as highly intellectual or scary. We approached him and he was interested to know more.

But Frank and Joan? What would that look like? What would it feel like? Would the two of them get along?

Sam, Dan and I arranged to take them both to lunch, and Frank told us later that he'd agreed to the meeting just because he liked the idea of seeing the words "lunch, Joan Bakewell" in his diary. We went to J. Sheekeys, just off the Charing Cross Road, and from the very first meeting the two of them got on like a house on fire. They presented both series together for three years before Frank felt he'd had enough, and we replaced him with the delightful Stephen Mangan. Stephen's relationship with Joan, and with everyone else on the team, was easy and friendly from the start.

Our next task was to cast the judges, which was never going to be easy, not least because the series was a whole new and unproven format so anyone coming aboard it would be committing an act of faith. Credibility in the sometimes rather precious art world is hard won and easily lost, and so we needed people with enough self-confidence to take the gamble.

In the mix we ideally wanted a curator, a dealer and an artist. Through a process of research and chatting and getting acquainted and then screen testing, we eventually alighted on Kathleen Soriano, who was at that time the Head of Exhibitions at the Royal Academy; Kate Bryan who was Head of Contemporary at the Fine Arts Society, and Tai Shan Schierenberg who was and is a highly respected and amazingly talented painter of portraits and landscapes. Among his many sitters have been Seamus Heaney and Her Majesty the Queen.

Our first port of call when we were developing the Portraits format was to Sandy Nairne who was at that time the Director of the National Portrait Gallery. Sandy warmly welcomed any idea which was likely to bring fresh debate and interest in portraiture, but was immediately sceptical that anything worthwhile could be produced within the four hours we planned to allocate for the artists to complete their artworks. "Maybe they could do a sketch in that time," he said. We took careful note of his comments but went ahead with our plan, and have found that as often as it's not enough time, four hours proves to be too much time and the artist can spoil a portrait by over-working it.

The NPG's initial encouragement extended to exhibiting the finalists' work in the gallery, which was an amazing achievement for the artists concerned and significantly boosted visitor numbers. However at that time the NPG was working with BP on its own portraits competition, and as our series gained popularity and momentum, so their freedom to cooperate with us was reduced.

The first episode of Portraits took place in a TV extravaganza in Trafalgar Square. We erected three huge marquees and put on a festival of painting which featured the competition at its centre, but also included sculpture, caricatures, exhibitions and masterclasses on all sides. The judges had whittled down the applicants to a short-list of twenty-one who appeared in that first episode (we soon realised that this was far too many), and our first sitters were Robert Lindsay,

211

Juliet Stevenson and Alison Steadman. It was a sunny day, there were huge crowds, and it all felt like a big success. We then took our road-show to Glasgow where we had another twenty-one artists and our sitters were John Hannah, Sophie Turner and the rugby star Michael Kerr, then on to Dublin, Cardiff and Paris where the finalists painted Sophie Dahl. The whole thing was a joy to make and a joy to watch. We were on a roll.

A TWIST

I could blame the stresses and strains caused by the loss of our child, or I could blame myself for always putting my work and career ahead of my family, or I could just take responsibility for my proven inability to be a loyal husband. One way and another however, after some thirty years, my marriage to Marilyn came to a painful end. None of the fault was hers, and all of it was mine.

My new friend and colleague Sam had been unhappy in her marriage for some while, but her reluctance to destabilise the lives of her two sons, Toby and Jonnie, had been enough to keep her family intact. Now she felt ready to make a break, and Sam and I began to make a life together. When both Toby and Jonnie were old enough to leave school, we bought a small apartment just a few hundred yards away from mine in Kingston, and while Sam moved in with me, the brothers were very happy to move in together just around the corner. In this arrangement Sam could continue to take every good care of them, still doing their cooking and cleaning, being there for them, but at the same time they could get a taste the independence most teenagers want. The boys and I were getting on well, and I badly wanted to avoid disputes which would inevitably end with "you can't tell me what to do – you're not my dad". Toby embarked on the early stages of a career in television, and Jonnie started on a course studying sound engineering and music production at the world-famous Abbey Road Studios.

Over a period of time we morphed into one of those modern extended families with some complicated arrangements with which everyone concerned has to learn to live. My daughter Alex took a while before she was willing to meet Sam, but when she did so, they began what would develop into a lovely new relationship for both of them. Alex had of course lost her only sibling much earlier in her life, and now she had acquired a new relationship with two boys that she happily started to refer to as her brothers. I had long since become used to having only one daughter, and now I began to get pleasure out of my developing relationship with Sam's two sons. I knew I should never try to replace their father; they still had one and were generally on good terms with him. However maybe I could provide another anchor for them as they set about navigating their new lives as more independent young men.

Sam and I learned how to sail, and at Christmas one year Toby and Jonnie came with us as we chartered a catamaran from St Vincent in the Grenadines, and sailed across to Mustique, Bequia and some of the other Windward islands. Neither of the boys turned out to be natural mariners, but both loved the sun, the sand and the warm seas. One day when we were transferring from the dinghy to the ladder on the stern of the cat, the boat keys were dropped and rapidly sank to the bottom. Quick as a flash, Toby swam down to the seabed with all the grace and ease of a dolphin, only to appear a few seconds later with a big smile on his face and holding the keys.

After a traumatic period of months going into years, it began to look as though life might settle down for a moment of calm. But a wise person once asked me the question, "Do you want to know how to make God laugh?" The answer? "Tell Him your plans."

THE BOOKS

I've referred several times to the fact that one of the many pleasures of TV production is the chance to work with a group of very talented people. If you can find great producers, a great director, great camera-operators, great sound recordists, brilliant designers, resourceful production managers, terrific floor managers, an amazing lighting crew, and then inspired editors and post-production team; if you find all those people, in the end you get to include your name in the closing credits of something which is far better than anything you could ever produce while working alone. Look at the closing credits of any Storyvault Films' show and you'll see a roll-call of some of the most talented people in the British television industry, and also the most affable. I feel very lucky indeed to be able to call them friends and colleagues.

But maybe it's been my lifelong fear of idleness, or maybe something more complicated, but I'm never completely satisfied unless I'm also doing something creative on my own. I've already mentioned the two novels published by Collins in the 1980s, and since then I've written five comedy books based on the Grumpy series, two more novels, (The Insect Farm and The Bridge) and three non-fiction books. The first of these is about the war in the Falklands and an unsolved political mystery called Secrets of the Conqueror. The second is called Black and Blue, and is the life-story of a remarkable woman I was fortunate to meet called Parm Sandhu.

I first met Parm through Marie-Elsa Bragg, whom I got to know because of my long-standing friendship with her dad. She told me about a project in which she wanted to interview a series of women from various ultra-orthodox religions. Their beliefs and customs are very different, but what all of them have in common is that they treat women as second-class citizens. Marie-Elsa wanted to record the interviews and make them available on-line.

Sam and I volunteered to help, and so we asked our friends Jon Woods and Georgia Cheales to lend a hand, and invited Marie-Elsa's group of women to our apartment in Kingston. We went ahead and recorded fascinating interviews with impressive women from the Muslim and Jewish communities, both of whom explained how women play a very special role within their religions, but that it is undoubtedly seen as an inferior one to that played by men.

Representing the Sikh religion, although she quickly pointed out that she was not devout or practicing, was a remarkable woman of Indian heritage called Parm Sandhu. At the time of the interview Parm was the most senior female officer of black or Asian background in the Metropolitan Police, and her history was extraordinary.

On that day, and then as part of a lasting friendship, I got to hear the astonishing story of Parm's life and her various struggles against every type of obstacle. Over the following weeks and months, she and her husband Rod would frequently be among guests at our dinner table. Everyone would do the "what did you do today?" or "how did you and your partner first meet?" type conversations, and whenever it got around to Parm, everyone else's jaws would drop. While all the rest of us had had a frustrating meeting with a commissioning editor or had to attend a boring presentation by the accounts team, Parm had been obliged to visit the scene of a murder. When we told our stories of meeting our eventual partners at work or in a pub, Parm told how she was forced into an arranged marriage when she was aged just sixteen, and met her first husband for the first time on her wedding day.

Over many weeks and months I would frequently tell Parm that she should write a book about her life. Always she would reply that she didn't have time, had signed the Official Secrets Act, and that her story wasn't all that remarkable. I responded that it certainly was, and that if she didn't feel able to write it, maybe she'd let me do so.

In the following months, Parm and I met for two hours once a week or so, a total of maybe twenty times. I left every one of those meetings shocked and disgusted by the continuous experience she had endured of racism and sexism, all set against the background of a working environment dominated by a group of middle-aged white men of a particular type. Many of the police officers concerned would not have been racist or sexist as individuals, but were part of a system which had justly been declared to be institutionally racist. From her very first day on duty when the area's elite driver had forced her out of the patrol car and abandoned her alone, late at night in an area notorious for street crime, to the end of her career when a spurious charge of gross misconduct was made against her and she had to fight to clear her name. When I put all this together end to end, and Parm read her full story for the first time, she cried. Her coping strategy throughout her life and career had been to compartmentalise each incident and setback, and always to move forwards. Only when she saw it all in a continuous narrative, did even she realise that her story added up to something extraordinary. The book is entitled Black and Blue, by Parm Sandhu, and I always ask people to buy and read a copy, and then give it to someone they know who is going through adversity. Parm is an inspiration.

I went along with Parm when she appeared at the Chiswick Book Festival to be interviewed by the estimable and rather brilliant Georgina Godwin. Georgina is one of the smartest people in the book world, and seemed to have genuinely enjoyed Black and Blue. In the course of chatting before the gig, she asked me if by any chance I knew Phil Manzanera. I'm a bit of a music nut in my spare time so I was ready with the answer.

"Obviously I know that Phil is the amazing guitarist from Roxy Music, and I know he's usually the other guitarist on stage alongside David Gilmour, but I don't know much more than that."

Georgina confirmed that Phil was about to celebrate fifty years in Roxy Music, but had also enjoyed an extraordinary career working with many of the world's all-time greats, such as David, Bob Dylan, David Bowie and scores of others. He was a friend of Georgina's and "he's looking for someone to help him to write his life-story."

I was immediately interested, and that evening I googled Phil and was astonished that I didn't already know more about him. He's had a diverse and fascinating life in rock and roll and Latin-American music and, most importantly, David Gilmour's wife Polly Sampson described him as "the second nicest man in rock." (I'm guessing that she doesn't think the nicest man is Roger Waters). Georgina kindly arranged a meeting, at which Phil and his wife Claire and I immediately hit it off. Hearing just a few of the headlines of his life was enough to convince me that there was a compelling book to be written. He'd been a small boy growing up in Cuba during Castro's revolution, and had memories of crouching down in the family bathroom as bullets flew over his head. He'd been invited to tea with Salvador Dali, and had played alongside David Gilmour at the famous concert in the shipyards at Gdansk. He'd had one of his guitar riffs sampled by Jay-Z and Kanye West, with astonishing consequences. I was really happy to help him to write it all down, and Phil's life-story, "From Revolucion (sic) to Roxy" is available in all good bookshops. Phil and Claire are now firm family friends. Thank you Georgina.

WORK-LIFE BALANCE

___

Living and working together with Sam worked well from the beginning and has continued to do so. Along with Danielle Graham, she and I are executive producers of Portrait Artist of the Year, but Sam's particular contribution to the latter has been to cast a veritable pantheon of interesting and distinguished sitters for our competing artists to paint. Over the years our sitters have included Eddie Marsan and Jodie Comer, Melvyn Bragg and David Tennant, Derek Jacobi and Anne Reid, Rory Stewart and Lesley Manville, Alastair Campbell and Judi Dench among literally hundreds of stars. The series winners have been commissioned to make portraits of Hilary Mantel, Sir Ian McKellen, Graham Norton, Tom Jones, Nile Rodgers, Alan Cumming, Kim Cattrall, Carlos Acosta, Nicola Benedetti, Sir Lenny Henry and Dame Jane Goodall, among many others. Their portraits are in the collections of the British library, the Walker Art Gallery in Liverpool, and the national galleries of Ireland, Scotland, Wales and the National Portrait Gallery. It was a source of particular pride and joy for me when I was able to fulfil the ambition I'd expressed when the programme was first commissioned. Joan Bakewell, aged ninety, co-presented and was the magnificent final sitter for the tenth series. What a woman!

The original idea had been that Sky would alternate Portraits one year and Landscapes the next, but the shows were so successful from the start that the channel asked us to make both in the same year. Of course the answer was yes, and every series we've made from that day to this has built new audiences and appreciation.

There has been equal joy and success in our productions of Landscape Artist of the Year, which have involved annual military-type manoeuvres running all around Britain and Northern Ireland. We've been on every coast from Trelissick in Cornwall to Whitstable in Kent, from the Gower peninsular in Wales to Fleetwood and Redcar, and from Blackpool in Lancashire to Cromarty in Scotland. And there's a similar and equivalent rollcall of honour for the series winners of the Landscapes series, which has produced artworks exhibited in The Imperial War Museum, The Manchester Art Gallery, The Maritime Museum in Greenwich, the Science Museum, the Royal Institute of British Architects, and the headquarters of the National Trust among others.

The other favourite aspect of producing Landscapes is that our recording outside on location means that alongside the eight pre-selected and featured artists, we are able to invite up to fifty "wild cards" – artists who didn't make it onto the short-list, but who come along to be part of the show, just for the joy of painting. They come from miles around, usually bringing a partner or friend to help carry their equipment (and especially a big umbrella), and they settle down on the grass or the sand, on riverbanks and cliff edges, and spend the day with us and our production team. Over the years this hardy band of happy artists have braved just about everything the British weather can throw at them, and then some more. On one occasion we were sited precariously on a cliff-edge in the west of Wales. The wind was howling like an angry ghost, the rain had been constant since dawn and showed no sign whatever of abating before nightfall. I watched as the wildcards and their friends and families struggled with tipping easels and umbrellas blowing inside out, and wondered how many would stay the course. After a while I walked among the crowds speaking in turn to little groups: "usually we spread the four hours of the competition over six hours so that everyone can have breaks, but in view of the weather, we wondered if you'd like to cut things a bit shorter today?" Every one of them without exception looked at me as though I had taken leave of my senses. "What?" they said, "we've come here to paint and we're going to paint." And they did, and at the end of the day we lined them all up and got the Steadicam to walk down in front of them, while we played "Land of Hope and Glory" on the soundtrack. The wild-cards are always a joy, and at the end of each recording day, our three judges select one overall winner from among the eight who will go forward to the semi-final, and then also one winner from among the wild-cards. When the six heats have all been recorded, the judges choose their favourite from all the wild-cards to join the other heat winners.

But the best, the very best thing about producing both of these series is when I meet artists who appeared in one or other of them maybe five years ago, and tell me "I've never stopped working since." Above all, struggling or aspiring artists just want and need to get their work seen, and so whether or not they progress in the competition, they're able to show their art to potential buyers. I know for a fact that scores of artists have had their careers transformed by appearing in Portraits or Landscapes, and that's a reason for celebration.

Our other source of joy and inspiration has been to work with terrific commissioning editors such as Benedetta Pinelli at Sky, and with outstanding producers such as the wonderful Anne Elletson, who was Editor of our long-running series of The Book Show with Mariella Frostrup. Among the many guests I was thrilled to meet was Harry Belafonte, who kindly admired the traditional flat cap I was wearing to keep out the persistent rain at the Hay Festival. I saw the opportunity and quickly swapped it for his baseball cap labelled UNICEF. Later Anne produced the Sky Arts' Book Club with Elizabeth Day and (one of my favourite presenters of all time) Andi Oliver. And before the BBC took almost all of their arts production in-house, Anne and the rest of us took enormous pride in producing some outstanding episodes of the Imagine strand, featuring everyone from Judith Kerr to Marlon James, from Colm Toibin to Howard Jacobson. Such happy days.

AND THEN ...

From an early stage in his life, Sam's oldest son Toby expressed enthusiasm for the military, and had been an exemplary member of the Air Cadets while still at school. He'd told his mum that he wanted to join the army after his A levels, but she was totally set against it, terrified of course that he'd be sent to some ghastly war zone. He was a brilliant skier, and he impressed us all when he set off for six months to work as a ski instructor in Japan. He still didn't know what he wanted to do when he came back, and to be fair to him, Toby did his best to settle into the various TV jobs we nudged him into. He came on and did well as a Runner on various of our productions of Landscapes, and although he enjoyed the energy and the camaraderie, it was probably never going to be the right fit. He loved motorbikes, which caused us enormous worry, but he took an advanced rider course and got a huge kick out of the freedom that having two wheels gave him. When he was twenty-one and told us that he had his heart set on joining the Marines, we realised there was little point in continuing to try to dissuade him. From the moment he knew he had our reluctant approval, he dedicated himself to the project with a level of enthusiasm we hadn't seen before.

It's well-known that the Marines' training courses and entry requirements are as tough as they come. Toby was a brown-belt in ju-jitsu, a PADI qualified deep-sea diver, and was fit and healthy;

and while he hadn't yet done much cardio or endurance exercise, he convinced himself that his grit and determination to keep going when others gave up would see him through.

On the afternoon of Tuesday 30th July 2019 I was on my way back from visiting Marilyn at her home in Hampshire. Our divorce was proceeding more or less amicably, we were on good terms, and I had driven down to see her to iron out some details. Sam had been to lunch with a work colleague and she called me shortly after I got home to say she was dropping into the boys' flat on her way. She'd called and texted Toby a couple of times earlier in the day and unusually he hadn't responded.

I was sitting at our kitchen table, working on my laptop just as I am at this moment when my phone rang again. I pressed the answer button and put it to my ear, and I heard Sam screaming.

"My son is dead. My son is dead."

I have come to believe that when something like this happens, the average person goes into a clinical state of shock, and for a while nothing they do quite makes sense. For some reason I cannot explain I said, "I'll be there in nine seconds." Only God knows why.

I hung up, leapt up, and instantly my mind was struggling to comprehend the words I'd heard. What had she said? It couldn't be right. It didn't compute. Maybe he had fallen down some stairs and was injured but still alive? Could he have been assaulted? Toby didn't use any drugs other than occasional weed, but maybe had accidentally taken an overdose of something and was unconscious but still breathing. What else could it be? Please God she hadn't found her son hanging. Of course not ... he was so happy and motivated. Mad thoughts, all a jumble, none of them making any sense. Whatever else, I knew I had to get there fast. I ran out of our apartment, down the outside staircase to the ground floor, and began to run through the streets towards their building. The distance is perhaps five hundred yards, and all the time my mind was whirling through possibilities, and all the time my lips were mouthing "no, no, no, no." For the entire journey I never once stopped mouthing "no, no, no, no." I felt my heart beating fast and fit to burst. I was sixty-eight and it was a while since I'd done much running, and the thought momentarily flashed through my mind that Sam was about to experience a double tragedy. In that short distance I remember hoping I wouldn't meet anyone I know because they would be concerned to see me in such a state and I wouldn't be able to stop to explain.

I ran up five outside stairs from the pavement to the front door, pushed the bell for flat three, and immediately heard the buzzer indicating that the door was unlocking. I continued to run up three long flights and found the apartment door open. Sam had called 999 and was speaking to the operator on the telephone. She gestured forward towards Toby's bedroom, where I could see him lying naked on the floor next to his bed with his head tilted forward, and instantly I knew there was no hope. I had seen enough dead bodies before and there could be no doubt.

Still I ran to him and crouched down alongside. The 999 operator was on speaker and asking all the well-known questions, urging us to look for any vital signs or perhaps to start CPR. A paramedic was on the way on a bike, apparently, and Sam was told to go to the front window to look out for her. She did, and within a few minutes she had arrived and I could hear her pounding up the stairway.

I looked into Sam's face for the first time and saw an expression I'd never seen before, one of shock and abject horror. Of course we were both completely stunned and had no idea what had happened. Toby was lying on his back with only a towel over his head. The towel had been covering his face when Sam found him, and she had instantly pulled it away in the hope that he was playing some sort of macabre game. His pallid skin and black lips left her in no doubt. She was still speaking on the phone and I heard her saying something like, "I've never seen a dead body before but I know that my son is dead."

The paramedic rushed into the bedroom as if to help, but instantly I could see that she knew there was no hope. Our beautiful twenty-two year old son Toby was lying dead on the floor, and there is no stronger or more profound feeling of powerlessness in the world. It was quite literally unbelievable, and yet here it was, in front of us, undeniable. If only you could put the clock back. If only you could unwind the course of events. If only you could undo it. How could this happen? How could this happen to Tobe? How could this happen to Sam, to us? How on earth could this happen to me? Twice.

Eventually, when every exhaustive final check had been done, the paramedic went with Sam into the living room to ask what she could tell her about the circumstances. I looked around and wondered. There were signs that he had probably just come out of the shower, and his pull-up bars were attached to the doorframe. Had he answered the door and been set upon, staggered backwards and broken his neck? There was no indication of a disturbance and no sign of bodily injury. I knew that I must not move him, but I placed my hand on the back of Tobe's head to try to find whether the skin was split, but could detect nothing untoward.

I could still hear Sam talking to the paramedic, recounting the story with amazing cogency, beginning from much further back than she'd want to know. How she had texted him the previous evening asking if he wanted anything from the supermarket. How she had phoned him several times during the day. How she had felt that something was wrong when she walked up the stairs and saw his motorbike padlocked outside. How she had let herself in, seen him lying on the floor ahead of her, and assumed he was playing some sort of joke. "Tobe? What are you doing?" She had called me, then called 999 and the rest she knew.

As I listened to her speaking, I sat quietly on the floor alongside Toby's dead body, gazing into his handsome face and wondering about the fragile and delicate thing which makes the vast and tragic difference between life and death. Here was this young man, on the brink of his new life, perfectly fit and healthy just a short while ago, but a spark of life had gone, and all of a sudden the vital, vivid, animated being that was him was an empty vessel. How elusive the thing we call life, and how complete and devastating is its absence in death.

An ambulance arrived, and then the police, and once again Sam patiently talked the constable through the series of events leading up to her discovery of her dead son. Obviously they had their job to do, ruling out what is euphemistically known as "foul play". Two of them had a quick look round.

"Did he use drugs?"

"Only rarely and only a little bit of weed."

They seemed satisfied, sympathetic and supportive.

As they finished up their business, it was now evening and Sam and I looked at each other, and held each other, utterly devastated by shock and disbelief. But then we quickly realised that Toby's father and brother needed to be the first to know what had happened. Jonnie and Toby were the closest brothers I have ever come across, and it didn't bear thinking about how he would react. He was staying with his dad on this evening, and so at least they would be together when they heard the news.

Sam's first two calls to Toby's father went unanswered. Eventually she sent him a text saying, "Please call me urgently," at which point he rang her back. When he came on the line, they had the heart-breaking conversation that no parents ever want to have. The stuff of nightmares. What has happened? How did it happen? When did it happen? Nothing makes sense. It can't be so. It cannot be true. It simply can't be true.

To this day I don't know what happened next, other than that Toby's younger brother Jonnie was with his dad at the time and must have learned the news immediately. Even if I had been there and witnessed it, I know I would be unable to find any words which would come close to describing his reaction. Shock. Disbelief. Devastation. Closedown. Nothing comes close.

Sam's next instinct was that she needed to call her mother who lived in Kent, her father who lives in Los Angeles and her sister who lives in France. By now it was ten o clock at night, and I persuaded her to wait until the morning. They could do nothing tonight and they may as well have some sleep before they were forced to share the nightmare.

Eventually a black private ambulance pulled up in the street outside and two men came up the stairs and into the flat carrying a sort of stretcher on wheels. I knew exactly the process, and told Sam to wait in the living room while I made sure everything went as we would want it to. As the two strong men struggled down the steep and tight staircase carrying the weight of a fit young man and the trolley, my mind went straight back to the time twenty years earlier when two men delicately handled the much lighter load of our daughter Sammy down the stairs from her bedroom in our house, and into the waiting van. Two dead children. The first had died in my arms, and now the second had died in his bedroom. The first of their deaths had been long expected, but still left us bereft and in a state of shock and madness. The second had come with no warning whatsoever, and I had absolutely no idea how on earth we were going to get through what was to come.

With nothing further to be done, Sam had an overwhelming urge to see and to hug her son Jonnie, and so we got in the car and drove thirty miles to his father's house in Hertfordshire. I waited outside while she went in. Of course nothing could give any comfort, but she was able to hold her remaining son at the end of the worst day of either of their lives.

It must have been well past midnight when Sam and I walked back to our own apartment. Arm in arm, supporting each other physically, doing our best to support each other emotionally. There was nothing left to be said that night, and I lay beside Sam as she curled up into a small tight foetal ball and silently cried herself to sleep.

I have long believed that bereavement causes a bout of temporary insanity which can last days and may last years, but that in that period no-one can be held fully accountable for their actions. It's part of the reason why we have invented ceremony, so that we have things to do to somehow distract us from the reality of what has occurred. In Sam's case, the insanity was characterised by periods of utter emotional meltdown at the depth and agony of her loss, punctuated by periods of almost uncanny calm and apparent reason, as she explained what had happened to each of her parents, to her sister, to her beloved Aunt Michelle, to our friends and colleagues. In most cases she told the entire story in what might have seemed inappropriate detail or at undue length. And of course after they were able to take on board something of the shock and horror of events, everyone's question was the same. "Why?" At that point we only knew that it hadn't been violent, it hadn't been drug-related, and that it must have been sudden. Tobe's phone had been fully charged and within a few inches of where he had fallen; he would have had no difficulty in summoning help if there had been any warning.

One of the many things I was dreading was how to let Marilyn know what had happened. An example of my own temporary insanity is that for a moment I considered sending a text, perhaps apologising for not having let her know that I had arrived home safely after visiting her the previous day and explaining the reason. I quickly realised that this was not okay. However my stupidity was still in the ascendant when she answered the phone and I said something like, "I'm afraid I have the worst possible news." "Oh my God, not Alex," she said. I felt instant guilt and regret. "No no, not Alex. She's fine. So sorry. That was stupid of me." "What then?" I went on to tell her that Sam had found her son Toby dead on the floor of his bedroom. We had no idea what had happened or why. Marilyn's instant reaction was of course shock and distress, and her first thought was for Sam. It isn't necessary to go into details, but Marilyn overflowed with her grief and empathy for what had happened. Anything she could do, she said, and later she did. Her second thought was for me; how was I coping? We talked and agreed that while I could provide no kind of solution to how anyone copes with something of this kind, I was a living example of how, when you think you will never be able to survive something, you find that you can. Perhaps Sam might eventually be able to take some sort of comfort or strength from that.

Temporary insanity. I'd arranged a business meeting in London later that afternoon, and Sam suggested that maybe I should still go to take my mind off things. Temporary insanity. I had agreed to write a programme proposal for something we were pitching to a broadcaster; it was due later that afternoon and I assured colleagues that I'd deliver it. Temporary insanity.

How also to tell our daughter Alex what had happened to her brother, so newly acquired and so quickly gone. Toby and she had developed a lovely and rather special relationship in a short time, and I knew she would be devastated. To lose a second sibling. Sam and I got in the car and drove to Kingston hospital where Alex has a very responsible job managing several departments. She knew that something bad had happened the moment she saw us waiting in the car park. The news was like yet another earthquake.

Along with trying to cope with all the emotional carnage following the bombshell, of course we agonised over what on earth could have happened. In puzzling through everything we could think of or imagine, we both recalled that the paramedic had said something about "it sounds like his heart," but that scarcely seemed possible. Both Toby and Jonnie had been fit and healthy all their lives. They'd avoided a lot of the coughs and colds which affect many children, had scarcely ever needed or taken antibiotics, had never needed to go to the hospital. The brothers were slim and strong and robust pictures of health, but now suddenly one of them was dead.

As other possible causes were gradually eliminated, we came to learn more about something called Sudden Arrhythmic Death Syndrome, or SADS. All of us have read news stories about apparently fit and healthy young people simply collapsing and dying with no warning or previous symptoms. Most famously in recent times, the sporting world held its breath while Bolton Wanderers' player Fabrice Muamba collapsed on the pitch during a football match. Only the proximity of a heart defibrillator and the presence in the crowd of a cardiologist saved his life, but otherwise he certainly would have died. Also in recent memory had been the story of David Frost's son Miles who had collapsed and died whilst out running. Sam and I buried ourselves in research and began to understand that there can be many causes of such tragedies, but that often they occur without warning, sometimes while the victim is sleeping, sometimes during or after exercise. It seemed that everyone we spoke to knew someone, or knew of someone, to whom something similar had happened. Just along the river from where we live in Kingston, flowers were still being laid at the spot where a fifteen-year-old schoolgirl Rosie Mitchell had died during rowing practice.

In the case of any sudden and unexplained death, the coroner needs to be involved, and Sam was asked if it was okay to send off Toby's heart for examination to see if it would provide the answer to what had happened. Meanwhile the possibility that he'd had some sort of genetic and inherited condition caused instant alarm in relation to Toby's brother Jonnie. We discovered that we were fortunate to live within the catchment area of Dr Mary Sheppard who is an internationally acknowledged expert in SADS. Sam and Jonnie embarked on a series of ever more sophisticated tests to try to detect signs of an arrhythmia, and happily both were eventually declared to be in the clear.

It was Mary Sheppard who told us that SADS is the third most common cause of death among the young, after road accidents and suicide. An extraordinary thought in itself, but she also believes that its true incidence is vastly under-reported. Any time you hear of someone crashing a car or a motorbike for no apparent reason, or someone falling off a ladder or scaffolding, or being found at the bottom of a swimming pool, the answer could be that their heart has stopped. Sam and I reflected that Toby's love of his motorbike had caused several people close to us to criticise her for allowing it. (As if she had much say in the determination of a 22 year old). However if he had crashed and died while riding his bike, it's likely that no-one would ever have known that his heart had simply stopped working.

Sam's grief for the loss of her son was deep and profound and agonising. Sometimes she could get through the day, to all outward appearance seeming to others to be calm and even on her way to coming to terms with what had happened. Many times our friends and colleagues would remark on how she seemed to be accepting and sanguine, and often to be more concerned at their distress following the loss than she was about her own. "I feel lucky to have had him for as long as we did," she would say, and I could see people marvelling at her wisdom and apparent calm. Once back at home, and when we were alone, her resolve would fail and she would cry and lament and ask why, and then night after night she would sob herself to sleep. Frequently her sleep would be disturbed by nightmares, horror-filled images as she relived the scene when she went into her son's bedroom and found him lying dead on the floor. Dozens of times I was awoken in the middle of the night by her screams, sometimes beginning with a whimper but quickly reaching a crescendo as though she herself was being murdered. As urgently as I could, I would reassure her that she was okay, that everything was alright, that she was safe. But of course nothing was okay. Nothing would ever be okay, because she will always have lost her first-born son. Most often Sam would return to sleep very quickly, but I'd be left lying wide awake, my heart beating fast from its instant "fear or flight" reaction to someone you love calling for help.

In the morning she would apologise – like she was having nightmares on purpose. Truth to tell I was only ever glad to be alongside her.

Our grief is permanent and profound, and it comes in many forms. You think it's about a deep and agonising sense of loss of someone you love. The sudden disappearance of a presence you've always assumed would remain a constant. A big hole in your universe, a dull ache in your chest, a difficulty in getting to the top of your breath. It is all of those things that you might have experienced or be able to imagine, but it is also many more.

In our case, a new concern quickly took its place alongside Sam's grief for the loss of Toby, as her younger son Jonnie began what would be his long and difficult journey to come to some sort of terms with the loss of his brother. This is his and their story rather than mine, so I am not entitled to tell it in detail. However what it meant for me and us was that many times Sam felt as though she had lost not one son but two. Jonnie still lived and had his home in the place where his beloved brother had died. He loved it because it reminded him of Toby, and he hated it because it reminded him of his tragedy.

We all got through Toby's funeral on some kind of autopilot. Our good friend the Rev. Marie-Elsa Bragg made the trip back from France to conduct the service and hundreds of people turned up, all of them still ashen-faced several weeks after the death which had brought them all together. Even four years later it is too soon to recount the occasion in detail, but suffice to say that it contributed little to the process of healing.

The sight of many thousands of graves and plaques and memorials of one kind or another made us wonder what we could do that would be some kind of tribute to Toby's short but brilliant life. "Many people in these circumstances start running marathons or organising 'bring and buy' sales," I said to Sam. "But we are TV producers. We make TV programmes. Let's do that." So between us we put together a proposal for a documentary highlighting the issue of SADS, and especially the case for screening young athletes. We did not ever intend to tell Toby's story; it was too raw for us to be able to guarantee anything resembling objectivity. However our personal involvement and commitment to the story got us through the door to see Beejal Patel at BBC3, and we were steered towards a talented young director called Lindsay Konieczny. She immersed herself in the story and eventually located the family of Lauren Mead who had recently died in her sleep aged nineteen. Lauren's brother Patrick was going through a process which was recognisably parallel to that being experienced by Toby's brother Jonnie. The programme was called My Sister's Silent Killer and may still be available on the BBC iPlayer.

As I write, it is twenty-seven years since we lost our daughter Sammy to cystic fibrosis, and in that time, thank God, modern medicine has produced a range of treatments, and the prognosis for sufferers has been transformed. Meanwhile it's just four years since we lost our son Toby to SADS. They say that lightning doesn't strike twice in the same place, but sometimes I wonder why two people who were standing so close to me were so cruelly struck down. Did I do something terrible in this or in a former life for which I am being punished? Is it the selfish things I've sometimes done in this life which justified the retribution? Obviously I know that this is egocentric nonsense. Even if there is any kind of "meant to be" out there manipulating the universe, he/she/it would hardly be likely to pick on two total innocents just to teach me a lesson. It's not about me. It's about everything that Sammy was and could have been, and about everything that Toby was and could have been. It's in our nature to seek meaning where there is none, but of course these are tragic, tragic losses, no part of anyone's plan or greater scheme, and are utterly capricious and meaningless. Which makes them so much worse. Much later on, Sam and some of her close friends would alight on a project which could at least give some meaning to what happened to Toby.

TREATMENT FOR INSANITY

———

I've written earlier about my belief that a tragedy in the family can often be followed by a period of temporary insanity, during which it's advisable not to make big or irreversible decisions. When our daughter Sammy died, Marilyn and I floundered around, finding ourselves sure that we should move house and then equally sure that we shouldn't; sure that I should give up work and then equally sure that to do so would be madness. In the end, fate intervened and we found ourselves buying a totally derelict but potentially lovely cottage in a small village called Breamore on the edge of the New Forest. We soon got into a routine of dashing up and down the A3 on Fridays and Sundays, and throwing ourselves bodily into the hard manual work involved in making the place first habitable and then desirable. Absolutely everything needed to be done, and we did damn nearly all of it ourselves. Marilyn recalls working in the garden until her hands were stiff, sore and scuffed, and she was physically exhausted, and then still going on to work some more. I guess it was classic displacement activity, but it changed our lives and for several years Cherry Tree Cottage was our small sanctuary providing an essential diversion from some of our sorrows.

When Sam and I lost Toby, I did at least have the advantage of seeing the madness coming, and knowing about one thing we could do partially to alleviate it. I always say there is no roadmap showing how to deal with bereavement, but there is a general sense of direction, and I am familiar with the compass points. I applied for an allotment on a site of two hundred run by a community collective in nearby Bushy Park. The stars aligned so that within three months, in January 2020, we were allocated a patch of ground covered in bedsprings and bricks and overgrown brambles and dead wood, which looked as though it had last been used for a re-enactment of the Battle of the Somme. I had a strong feeling that once again the sheer physical tasks, and the focus on a project which was completely outside of our recent experience, might help just a bit.

The plan was that we would proceed slowly, maybe taking the plot a small section at a time, clearing an area and planting. Working a day each weekend, perhaps it would take a year or possibly two to sort everything. Then came Covid and lockdown and instead of visiting the allotment once a week, we began visiting every day. We threw ourselves into the tasks with total commitment and gradually a desolate patch of ground became our personal pharmacy. The healing effects of cutting and weeding and tilling and planting, the sheer visceral pleasure of putting hands deep into the soil. We built raised beds, laid paths, assembled compost bins, spread shingle, erected a shed, built a fruit-cage, planted seeds and seedlings, and then began to reap harvests of beans and beetroot and potatoes and onions and peppers and aubergines and lettuce and cucumber and courgettes and garlic and asparagus and rhubarb and on and on it goes, and I think our allotment plot five hundred yards away from our apartment in Bushy Park has possibly saved our lives. (Last year, we even came third in the competition for best plot.)

Having saved our lives, our work on the allotment continues to provide succour and satisfaction, and enables us to bore anyone who will listen about the inside leg measurement of the recent paimpol bean crop, or our experience with tromboncino courgettes. We worry that the damp weather may cause tomato blight, and we find ourselves handing our surplus cucumbers and courgettes to passers-by on our way home. Post Covid, the waiting lists have gone crazy, but take my advice and put your name down. Tilling the soil is good for you.

It's now three years since Sam and I were married, and four years since we lost Toby. For much of that time we've been thinking about whether there's something we can do that would feel appropriate as a permanent memorial to him. I've said before that somehow or other, yet another plaque on a wall of remembrance doesn't seem right for such a young person, and we don't feel any need for a physical structure to help us to remember him. Gradually and through lots of conversations with her close and longstanding friends, Sam has set up a community interest company, which is effectively a "not for profit" which they have rather brilliantly called Tobe-Heartsafe. The core idea is to encourage private schools and elite sports clubs to pay to have all their young people screened for the cardiac abnormalities which are so often resulting in tragedy. A team of cardiac nurses and a consultant cardiologist will be on hand so that if anything unusual is picked up, there can be an immediate expert assessment of whether the problem is real or not. But then the genius of the idea is that, for every screening which is paid for by the parents or the school or the sports club, Tobe-Heartsafe will arrange and carry out another screening on a young person who can't afford to fund it themselves. It's a sort of "buy one get one free" for saving lives.

Equally importantly, Sam's CIC is encouraging and providing CPR and defibrillator training in schools and offices, and is actively lobbying Parliament so that such training should become far more widely available. Every time the screening service arrives, or spreads the word in any way, Tobe's name and photo are clearly in evidence. Of course we will never know how many other families may be saved from going through the same tragedy that ours has gone through, but if it's one, or a handful or scores or eventually hundreds, Tobe-Heartsafe seems to us to be an appropriate way to sustain the memory of our beautiful boy.

AND FINALLY ...

———

It would seem appropriate, after half a century working in television, to impart a few thoughts on the state of the industry as I found it, versus how I find it today. Certainly there have been enormous changes since I began my life in it in 1974 – the biggest of them perhaps coming under the general heading of democratisation. When I joined the BBC, new entrants were drawn from a very narrow clique; there were exceptions, but generally you had a distinct advantage if you were white, male, had no regional accent, and had a decent degree from a top flight British university. It also helped if you had a familiar sounding surname. To join ITV at that time, you needed to have a union card from the ACTT, and you could only get a card if you had a job. Catch 22. For the vast majority of people, nepotism or other special access were the only ways in. The remarkably privileged jealously guarded their remarkable privilege.

Over the decades, the advent of Channel 4, then 5, then multi-channels, then services delivered on-line, has widened the access points for a whole range of people who otherwise would never have had a look in. When I look around the Storyvault Films' office at times of full production, it's positively joyous to experience people from every age and background. Opening up the catchment pool has immeasurably improved every aspect of our industry.

But there is still a long way to go. Even now, tight and prescriptive production budgets do not allow us to pay enough to enable the newest entrants to our industry to live a decent life in London, especially if they have dependents. This means that one way or another, anyone coming in for the first time has to be subsidised by their families, which in turn excludes so many of the people whose contributions we so badly need. If we're serious about wanting the TV workforce to reflect wider society, we have to address the issue in a much more planned and determined way.

Having said that the proliferation of routes to audiences is generally a good thing, it would be naïve to think there hasn't been a price to pay. Even with the advent of pay television in all its forms, the financial resources available to fund quality productions have not expanded at the same rate as the outlets competing for them. Production budgets are constantly being squeezed, and it's many years since ITV gave up resourcing the costly investigative current affairs teams at World in Action from Granada, The Cook Report from Central, and This Week from Thames.

With only the rarest of exceptions, investigative current affairs on television scarcely exists. Even the briefest canter through the areas I delved into during my five years as World in Action producer – including dodgy politicians, dodgy businessmen, dodgy dentists, and drug dealers – adds up to a catalogue of subjects that nowadays I never see on our screens – and I was one of ten producers on the team, many of whom were far more intrepid than I. Those kinds of bad guys have not gone away, but now they operate largely without fear of being confronted by a determined investigative reporter with accompanying film crew. The days of well-resourced journalists holding politicians and business to account, week in week out, are long behind us, and in a post-truth world, this is seriously to the detriment of our democracy.

Recent developments in the United States, where hopelessly partisan news channels have distorted news outrageously, have led to political divisions which are deeper and more dangerous than ever before. If we needed a demonstration of what happens when you impoverish and undermine a publicly funded national broadcaster, and allow special-interest "news" on TV, the consequences could scarcely be more clear; a political arena which is more ugly and divided than at any time in history, and Donald Trump. And yet no British political party seems to have the simple common sense necessary to support the BBC properly – either financially or by restoring and reinforcing its independence. The long term erosion of resources for a regulated news service dedicated to public service, as well as to the BBC World Service, are possibly the stupidest decisions by our politicians I've ever seen – and that's a very hard competition to win.

And our losses are not confined to the absence of proper account-ability and scrutiny. In the days of regulated broadcasters, a documentary or series featuring Harry and Meghan would have been obliged to approach and get interviews with the many people whose reputa-tions were smeared by casual and unfiltered criticisms. If the accused declined to appear, the producers would still have been required fairly to reflect their perspectives. Equally, the requirements for balance would have made it not okay to segue preposterously from Meghan's uncorroborated allegation of casual racism in the Royal Family to a brief history of slavery carried out by the British Empire. In the same way, Arnold Schwarzenegger would not have been free to fund a three-part revisionist history of his personal life, which air-brushed so effectively over his record of misogyny, without the inclusion of some balance. In the unlikely event that a documentary maker had been commissioned by a regulated broadcaster to make a four-parter about David and Victoria Beckham, or three hours about Coleen Rooney and "Wagatha", they would be unlikely to have so neatly skated over aspects of their lives which spoke of them less favourably.

My point is that in the new unregulated world of multi-platforms and streamers, if you have enough money, you can re-write your own history. Irritating and sometimes downright frustrating though they were, the IBA, then ITC, then Ofcom, used to ensure that what we saw on our television screens had gone through an editorial process which had some kind of integrity, objectivity and fairness. Now it's open season for anyone with the resources or ability to distort the world as it's beamed into our living rooms. Coming as it does at a time when a competent schoolboy or girl with the right kit can produce a video which makes it look as though a world leader or candidate is saying the opposite of what he or she is actually saying, I firmly believe we are sleepwalking towards disaster. A lie is halfway around the world before the truth has got its boots on, and this was never more the case than it is today.

And on a more personal note? This is where we came in. Everything that goes around comes around? Does it? Obviously none of us can really know, unless of course we get to look back from the next life. From the perspective of today, I always feel that my life so far has been full of amazing and brilliant pieces of good fortune. Living at this time, in this place, with reasonable health, reasonable prosperity, a good career, good friends and surrounded by people I love. I have been on the receiving end of some extraordinarily lucky breaks, and by any standards I must have been more favoured by the heavens than 99.99 per cent of all the people who've lived since the dawn of time. And yet ... and yet ... the tragedies which have befallen some of the people closest to me, especially of course Sammy and Toby, continue to inflict the pain of loss every single day of my life. How can someone who has lost two children count themselves as lucky? I am merely collateral damage, but nonetheless, it's damage. I am damaged.

And how can or should I respond to my injuries? The best way I ever get to understand it all, and explain it to the kids, is that we're all dealt a hand at birth, and then we continue to get random new cards throughout our lives. There's no point in saying "that's not fair" when someone else seems to have started off with all the aces, and it's also not a good idea to believe that a run of good cards is due to our own skill or virtue. Someone out there is dealing them, and whatever you get, that's what you get. We can't have any influence on the cards we're given; all we can do is to play them as well as we can. Don't complain, don't make excuses, just make the best you can of the cards in your hand. If you can do that, when you feel that twinge in the area around your heart as you are pushing a heavy wheelbarrow, at least you'll know you did your best.

Acknowledgements

I owe an enormous debt of gratitude to so many people, and hopefully I've managed to credit most of them without the narrative reading too much like an extended acceptance speech for a lifetime achievement award. However there are others whose names simply cannot be absent from a memoir of my fifty years in broadcasting, and even then I will have missed out some people who've given me a leg up or otherwise been in my corner.

These include the former Olympic swimmer and latterly deputy news editor at BBC Newcastle Ronnie Burns, from whom I learned so much. There's my friend and colleague Peter Hayton, who helped to make life in the Newcastle newsroom such great fun. Also John Blake, who was a colleague on World in Action and latterly was my deputy when commissioning factual programmes at ITV. My outstanding Chief Technology Officer at ONdigital, Simon Dore suffered a major stroke several years ago which put him out of action, but he remains a good friend. It was a treat to work alongside talented women such as Dianne Nelmes, Claudia Rosencrantz and Nicola Howson when I returned to the Network Centre as CEO. One of the former secretaries at World in Action, Marian Woods, became my first and only PA, and was a loyal and invaluable assistant throughout all my years as a suit.

Over the years I've dealt with a great many lawyers, but none of them has been more thorough and committed than the marvellous

Rowena Cordrey, who kindly read this book for me, and has hopefully kept me out of trouble.

Brilliant producer/directors in the twenty two years as an independent have included Anna Thompson and Alan Lewens, and the undiluted joy of making our recent hit shows, "Portrait Artist of the Year" and "Landscape Artist of the Year", has been immeasurably enhanced by working with Series Editors such as Amanda Westwood, Fiona Cleary, Marina Fonseca, Nelda Sale, Charlie Sever, and all of their teams.

While the creatives tend to get most of the limelight, nothing worthwhile can ever be achieved without excellent support professionals, and our Production Manager at Liberty Bell Judy Lewis was the exemplar of calm efficiency, and our Unit Manager for several years at Storyvault, Ali Brodie was equally marvellous. Meanwhile the inimitable Matt McShane has consistently made sure that our bills are paid on time.

In composing this memoir, I've benefitted from the wisdom and advice of several people, most notably my good friends Janet Reibstein, Anne Elletson and Olivia Lichtenstein. Thank you.

And of course nothing at all would be possible without Alex, Jonnie and Sam.

That's still left out a great many people who deserve credit, some of whom will no doubt find a subtle way of making me feel guilty, and to whom I of course apologise. After all, it's far too late to make new old friends.

By the same author

A Power in the Land

The Lazarus File

Grumpy Old Men: The Official Handbook

Grumpy Old Men: The Secret Diary

Grumpy Old Christmas

Grumpy Old Drivers

Grumpy Old Workers

The Insect Farm

Secrets of the Conqueror

The Bridge

Black and Blue (with Parm Sandhu)

About the Author

Stuart Prebble has worked in television since he left Newcastle University in 1974 (sic) where he studied Anglo-Saxon as a modern language. He joined the BBC as a journalist and on-screen reporter, and was briefly famous in the north-east - even once hosting an entertainment spectacular in Blyth. He went on to produce and edit ITV's World in Action current affairs series, and was ITV's first Commissioning Editor for Factual programmes. He was nominated for the BAFTA and had to try to look happy when he didn't win it, but was consoled by winning the RTS award for Best Factual Series. Stuart was eventually enticed to wear a suit, and rose through the ranks to become Chief Executive of ITV. He left in 2002 to set up an independent production company, Liberty Bell, where he originated and produced shows like the (various) Grumpies, Three Men in a Boat, the Alastair Campbell Diaries and many more. Then in 2012 he joined with friends to establish Storyvault Films, which makes terrific Arts and documentaries for all the decent channels. He is the author of thirteen published books.

Milton Keynes UK
Ingram Content Group UK Ltd.
UKHW020036050724
445034UK00015B/262

9 781783 243191